UAE
road atlas

The **Complete A to Z** Road Atlas

there's more to life...
ask**explorer**.com

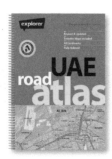

UAE Road Atlas 3rd Edition ISBN 13 - 978-9948-450-10-8

Copyright © Explorer Group Ltd 2013.
Maps Slobodan Radovanovic, MAGIC MAP.
All rights reserved.
Printed and bound by Emirates Printing Press, Dubai, United Arab Emirates.

Explorer Publishing & Distribution
PO Box 34275, Dubai
United Arab Emirates
Phone   +971 (0)4 340 8805
Fax   +971 (0)4 340 8806
Email   info@ask**explorer.**.com
Web   ask**explorer.**com

Contents

Welcome...

Welcome to the Explorer's **UAE Road Atlas**.

This product is unique and much needed; it is the only atlas to cover the whole of the UAE. All the major roads, developments, wadis, wells, malls, souks, camel tracks and hotels that dot the country are marked.

The map index on the inside front cover shows the areas covered by each map, while a full legend and other useful information can be found on the flap on the back cover. For an explanation of what the grids and all the other information on the maps mean, turn to page IV.

The Explorer Team

For more information about Explorer products see the back section.
Explorer has long provided UAE residents with the best maps and guidebooks available. From the Mini Guides and Residents' Guides to the popular Mini Map series, Explorer Publishing has the UAE covered.

Of course, this country is developing at a phenomenal rate, and new projects are popping up all the time. If you notice that a road has closed, a track has opened, or another development is rising from the sands, let Explorer know by logging on to askexplorer.com or email us at maps@askexplorer.com.

A To Z Of UAE Driving

The general standard of driving in the UAE is not good. Drivers often seem completely unaware of other cars and drive too fast, too close, swerve erratically, pull out suddenly or drift mindlessly across lanes. The most important advice for drivers is to stay alert. However, standards are improving, and the following A to Z of hints and tips should set you on the right path.

Accidents

All accidents must be reported to the police. If it is serious, dial 999 for emergency help. For minor collisions that do not require emergency services to attend, call the police in the relevant emirate (see back cover flap for numbers).

If there is only minor damage, and the vehicles are blocking traffic, they can be moved to the side of the road. Be warned that there is no clear definition of what constitutes 'minor damage' and you can also be fined for illegally moving your vehicle after an accident. The police control room will be able to give you guidance when you phone to report the incident.

If there is any doubt as to who is at fault, or if there is an injury (however slight), do not move the cars. If you do, the police may hold you liable should anything then happen to that person. Once the police arrive, they will assess the accident and apportion blame on site. It can be an unscientific process, and there's no right of reply if you disagree. You should calmly, politely and firmly give your account of events. This may be a good chance to try your Arabic pleasantries.

The police will provide a copy of the accident report. Submit this to your insurance company to get the vehicle repaired. A pink report means you are considered at fault, and green means you are the inncocent party.

The number of accidents rockets during the holy month of Ramadan, as many drivers are tired, hungry and in a rush to get home in the late afternoon and evening. Also, beware of animals (typically camels) crossing more remote roads.

Better Driving

Keep The Hard Shoulder Clear

NEVER drive along the hard shoulder. Not only is it very dangerous, it is also ILLEGAL.

Keep Right

ALWAYS move over as far right as possible, as soon as it is safe to do so.

Keep Your Distance

NEVER drive too close to the vehicle in front. Always leave at least a three second gap between you and the next vehicle.

Box Junctions

NEVER enter a box junction until your exit is clear.

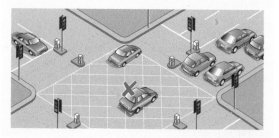

Blood Money

As the law currently stands, the family of a pedestrian killed in a road accident is entitled to Dhs.200,000 diya (blood money). This is usually paid by the insurance company, unless the driver was under the influence of alcohol. Blood money is not automatically due if the victim was walking across a road not intended for use by pedestrians, such as Sheikh Zayed Road.

Breakdowns

In the event of a breakdown, pull your car over to a safe spot until help arrives. For recovery services, see the back cover flap.

Children

Children under 10 years old are not allowed to sit in the front of a car.

Further Information

For complete information on safety and road rules, check out the Safe Driving Handbook available from the Emirates Motor Sports Federation, or police websites (see Useful Information on the back cover flap).

Insurance

Most UAE insurance is not valid for travel into Oman or trips into the desert. For the former, try Oman Insurance (800 4746) or, if crossing at Hatta, there are booths near the border offering coverage for around Dhs.150 for a weekend.

Mobiles

Using handheld mobile phones while driving was banned in 2007. This is still widely ignored, but pull over or use a hands-free set to ensure you avoid a fine.

Petrol Stations

Petrol stations in the UAE are run by Emarat, EPPCO and ENOC (ADNOC in Abu Dhabi). Most offer extra services, such as a car wash, snacks and a convenience store. Many have a 'cash only' policy, so make sure you have money to hand before you fill up, and don't rely on there being an ATM.

Radio

Avoid a traffic jam by tuning in to any of the following radio channels: Al Arabiya (98.9FM), Al Khallejiya (100.9FM), Dubai 92 (92.00FM), Coast (103.2FM), Dubai Eye (103.8FM) Channel 4 (104.8FM), Emirates 1 (99.3 or 100.5FM) and Emirates 2 (99.3 or 106FM). The BBC World Service can be picked up on 90.3FM in Abu Dhabi and 87.9FM in Dubai.

Road Rules

In the UAE, you drive on the right hand side of the road. Dubai has its own police force, and rules vary slightly between there and the other emirates. For finer details about road rules, have a look at the police website in your emirate (see Useful Information on the back cover flap).

Safer Driver

This firm will send a driver to you if you've taken your car out and decided to have a drink. He will then drive your car home (with you in it) and be on his merry way. Call 04 268 8797 to book. (saferdriver.ae)

Salik

In 2007, the Salik road toll system came into effect in Dubai. It has four gates, one on the Garhoud Bridge, one on Sheikh Zayed Road near Mall of the Emirates, one on Sheikh Zayed Road near the Al Safa Interchange, and one on the Maktoum Bridge. There are no booths, and no need to stop as you drive through. Instead, drivers stick a tag to their windscreen, which is read by radio frequency as they pass. It costs Dhs.4 each time. Those that don't have a card will be fined Dhs.100. The kit can be bought from most petrol stations. Visit salik.ae or call 800 72545 for more information.

Seatbelts

It is mandatory to wear seatbelts in the front seats.

Speed Limits

Speed limits are usually 60kph to 80kph around town, and 100kph to 120kph on major highways. The speed limit is clearly indicated on road signs. Speeding fines begin at Dhs.400 for driving up to 10kph over the limit. Parking fines start at Dhs.100. Both come with black points. You can also be fined Dhs.100 on the spot for being caught driving without your licence. Fixed and movable radar traps across the country (and police patrols) catch the unwary. In 2009, traffic fines collected by the Dubai Police crossed the Dhs.1 billion mark. In most cases, you won't know you've received a fine until you check on the police website for your emirate or renew your vehicle registration.

Swearing

Rude gestures, like extending your middle finger, can lead to prison, as can giving other drivers an earful of abuse.

Violations

If you wish to report a traffic violation, call the Traffic Police's toll free hotline (800 4353). Abu Dhabi and Dubai Police have useful websites (see Useful Information on the back cover flap) with details of traffic violations, road maps and contact numbers.

Zero Tolerance

Police in the UAE exercise a strict zero tolerance policy on drinking and driving. This means that if you have had anything to drink, you should not get behind the wheel. If you get into an accident, whether responsible or not, and fail a blood-alcohol test, you will probably be held in custody until trial and are then likely to face prison. In addition, your insurance is automatically void. Police have increased the number of random drink-driving checks. You should also be aware that alcohol may still be in your system from the night before.

Product Customisation

Explorer products can be customised and used as corporate gifts, orientation packs for new staff, or promotional giveaways. Clients can add a new cover designed to meet their branding guidelines, or add a new cover image. Copy and contact details can be added to the back cover, advertisements placed inside, pages inserted, changes made to the colour scheme, a welcome message added, and new locations (with contact details) placed on maps.

Regular Explorer cover

Regular Explorer cover

New cover image

Company logo

New cover image

Company logo

Samples of previous customised covers

Regular Explorer cover

New cover image

Company logo

3D Maps

Explorer can also provide customised 3D maps. These act as an excellent visual guide to an area, but can also include comic touches and tiny slice-of-life details.

There are two significant advantages to using 3D maps. Firstly, their similarity to the physical world means that even the most map-phobic people can understand them and, secondly, the scope for creative flourishes is unlimited. Corporate clients may choose to include logos (a streetside billboard, a branded plane flying across the city) or examples of their business in action (smiling customers receiving their goods, staff on their way to work).

For more information on any of these options please go to askexplorer.com

Location Maps

Explorer's maps cover the whole of the UAE, and major cities in the Arabian Gulf and throughout the world.

These products are well known and relied on by people across the globe. The maps highlight local landmarks, museums, hospitals, schools, malls, markets and other areas of interest. They are also an invaluable tool for finding your way around.

If people can't find you, they can't buy your products or services. Maps for any city that Explorer has covered can be customised to help clients get to you. Explorer covers all the GCC capital cities, along with commercial hubs in Asia (Beijing, Shanghai, Hong Kong, Singapore, Sydney), North America (New York, LA, Vancouver) and Europe (London, Paris, Barcelona, Dublin, Amsterdam, Berlin).

These can be printed in any format you want, from business cards to laminated posters, or as a PDF for email.

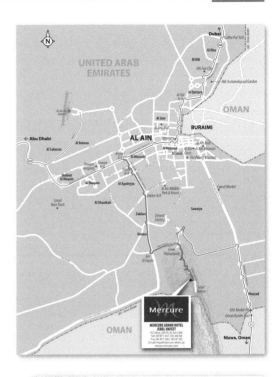

Wall Maps

If there's a part of the planet that is particularly important to you, we can create a poster of it. Our maps cover major cities across the world, any of which can be blown up as wall maps in your chosen size. Just choose the area you're interested in, and decide if you'd like an overview or greater detail. Then, opt for landscape or portrait and pick any size you want.

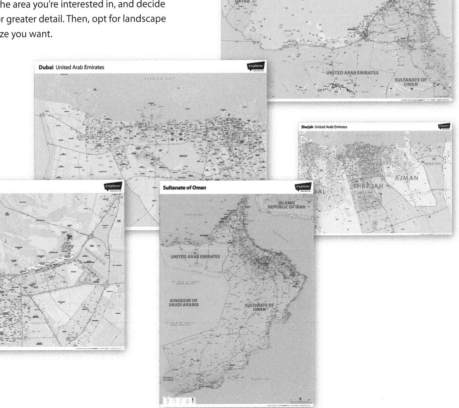

UTM Zone 40R

QATAR

UNITED ARAB
EMIRATES

SAUDI
ARABIA   OMAN

ARABIAN GULF

Khasab

MUSANDAM
(SULTANATE OF
OMAN)

ARABIAN GULF

Ras Al Khaimah

Umm Al Quwain
Ajman
Sharjah
Dubai

Dibba

Dhaid

Khor Fakkan

Fujairah

Jebel Ali

Madam

Hatta

ABU DHABI

UNITED ARAB
EMIRATES

SULTANATE
OF OMAN

Al Ain

| | A | 400,000 E | 56° 00′ | | B | 410,000 E | | C | 56° 10′ | | 420,000 E | | D |

1

26° 20′

2,910,000 N

ARABIAN GULF

2

To Bandar A Bas (Iran)

Ra's Shaykh Mas'nd

Alila Villas
Musandam (u/c)

Al Harf

Hana

3

2,900,000 N

Al Jiri   **Tawi**

Strait of Hormuz

²¹Golden Tulip
Khasab Hotel

Mukhi

Lake Hotel

Qida **Khasab**

11.2

Khasab Airport

Khasab Hotel

26° 10′

4

Dam

Bukha

Dam

Bukha Fort

8.6

3

2,890,000 N

Fudgha

1.8

Ghumdah

△
1360

5

5.3

Tibat

O M A N

3.6

| A | 400,000 E | 56° 00′ | B | 410,000 E | ▼ 3 | C | 56° 10′ | 420,000 E | D |

© Explorer Group Ltd. 2013

Scale 1: 190,000 1 cm to 1.9 km

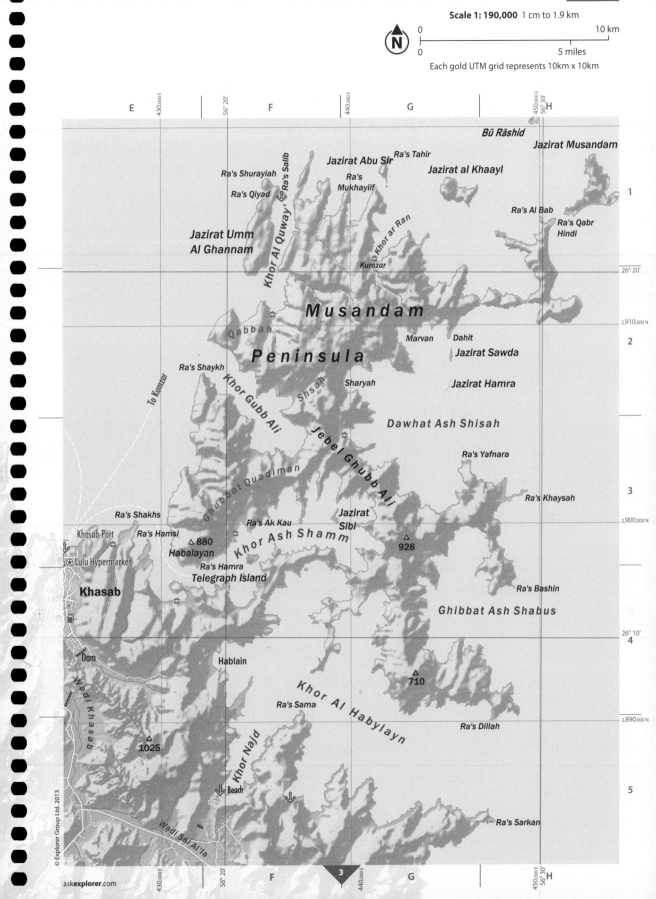

Each gold UTM grid represents 10km x 10km

Bū Rāshid

Jazirat Musandam

Jazirat Abu Sir   Ra's Tahir

Ra's Shurayiah   Ra's Salib   Jazirat al Khaayl

Ra's Qiyad   Ra's   Ra's Al Bab
                   Mukhaylif
                                     Ra's Qabr
Jazirat Umm   Hindi
Al Ghannam   Khor Al Quway   Khor ar Ran

                                   Kumzar

Musandam

                  Qabbah   Marvan   Dahit
Peninsula   Jazirat Sawda
Ra's Shaykh
                  Khor Gubb Ali   Sharyah   Jazirat Hamra
                         Shsah
                                   Dawhat Ash Shisah
              Jebel Ghubb Ali
                                   Ra's Yafnara

          Ghubbat Quadiman   Ra's Khaysah

Ra's Shakhs
                   Ra's Ak Kau   Jazirat
Khasab Port   Ra's Hamsi   Sibl
                        △ 880   △
Lulu Hypermarket   Habalayan 928
                   Ra's Hamra
Khasab   Khor Ash Shamm
                   Telegraph Island   Ra's Bashin

                                   Ghibbat Ash Shabus

Dam   Hablain
                                   △
Wadi Khasab   Khor Al Habylayn   710

               Ra's Sama
                              Ra's Dillah
△
1025   Khor Najd

        Beach   Ra's Sarkan

Wadi Sal Al'ia

UTM Zone 40R

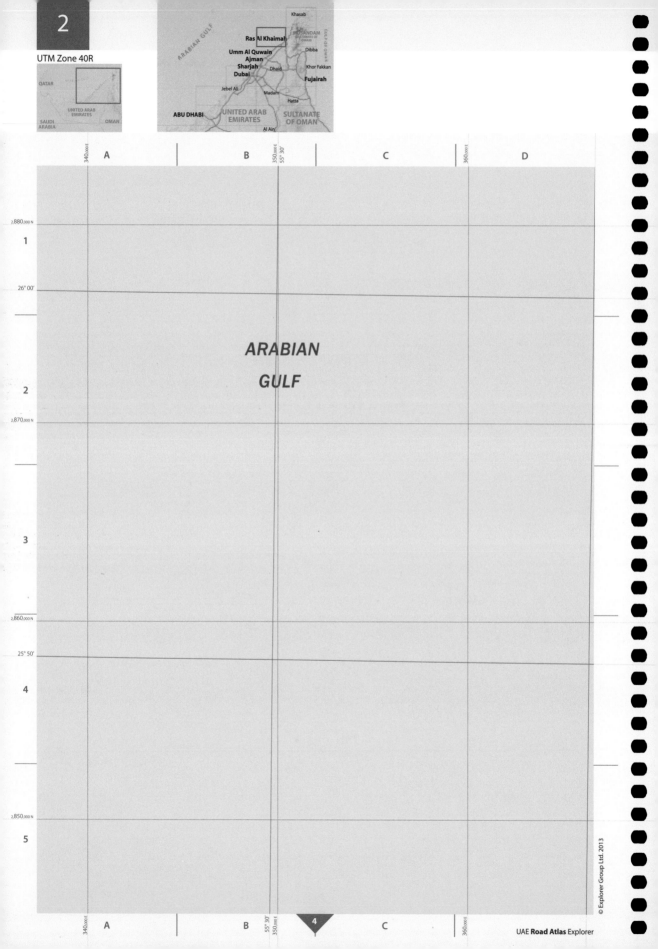

ARABIAN

GULF

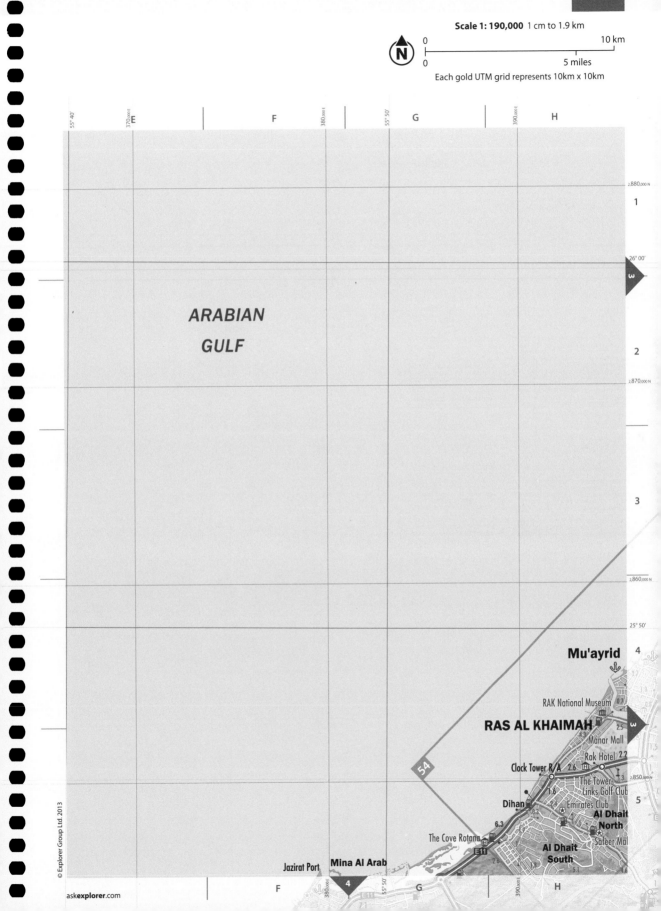

Scale 1: 190,000 1 cm to 1.9 km

Each gold UTM grid represents 10km x 10km

ARABIAN

GULF

Mu'ayrid

RAK National Museum

RAS AL KHAIMAH

Manar Mall

Rak Hotel 2.2

Clock Tower R/A

The Tower
Links Golf Club

Dihan

Emirates Club

Al Dhait North

Safeer Mall

The Cove Rotana

Al Dhait South

Jazirat Port

Mina Al Arab

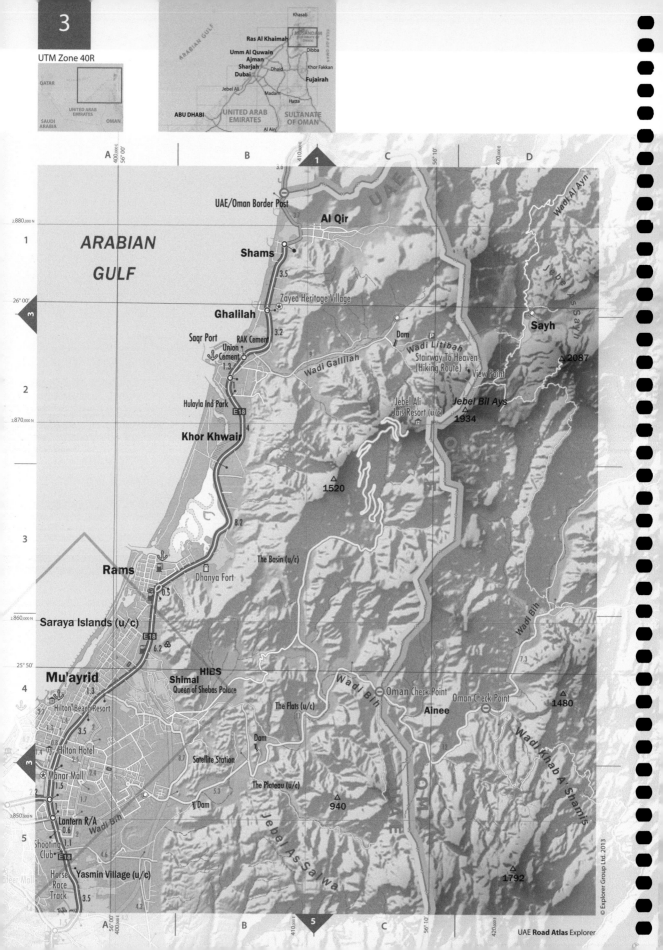

3

UTM Zone 40R

QATAR

UNITED ARAB EMIRATES

SAUDI ARABIA   OMAN

ARABIAN GULF

Khasab

MUSANDAM (EMIRATE OF OMAN)

Ras Al Khaimah
Umm Al Quwain
Ajman
Sharjah
Dubai   Dhaid

Dibba

Khor Fakkan

Fujairah

Jebel Ali   Madam   Hatta

ABU DHABI   **UNITED ARAB EMIRATES**   **SULTANATE OF OMAN**

Al Ain

A   B   C   D

1

UAE/Oman Border Post

Al Qir

3.7

Shams

3.5

Zayed Heritage Village

1

2,880,000 N

ARABIAN
GULF

26° 00'   **3**

Ghalilah

3.2

Saqr Port   RAK Cement
Union Cement
1.3

Hulayla Ind Park
E18

Khor Khwair

4

8.2

Dam

Wadi Galilah

Wadi Al Ayn

Wadi Litibah
Stairway To Heaven
(Hiking Route)
View Point

Jebel As Sayh

Sayh

△2087

Jebel Ali
Jais Resort (u/c)

Jebel Bil Ays
1934

△
1520

2

2,870,000 N

3

Rams

Dhanya Fort   The Basin (u/c)

0.3

Saraya Islands (u/c)

E18
6.2

25° 50'   **4**

Mu'ayrid

1.3

Hilton Beach Resort

3.5

Hilton Hotel

Manar Mall

1.5

2.2   1.7

Lantern R/A
0.6

Shooting
Club   1.1

E18   4.6

Horse
Race
Track   3.5

HIBS
Shimal
Queen of Shebas Palace

The Flats (u/c)

Dam

Satellite Station   8.7

The Plateau (u/c)   5.3

Dam

Wadi Bih

Wadi Bih   Oman Check Point

Ainee

Oman Check Point

△
1480

△
940

Wadi Khab A'Shamis

Jebel As Salwa

△
1792

2,860,000 N

2,850,000 N

3

5

A   B   5   C   D

Wadi Bih

4.3

3.0

7.3

12

△
56° 00'   56° 10'   56° 10'

© Explorer Group Ltd. 2013

UAE Road Atlas Explorer

Scale 1: 190,000 1 cm to 1.9 km

0   10 km

0   5 miles

Each gold UTM grid represents 10km x 10km

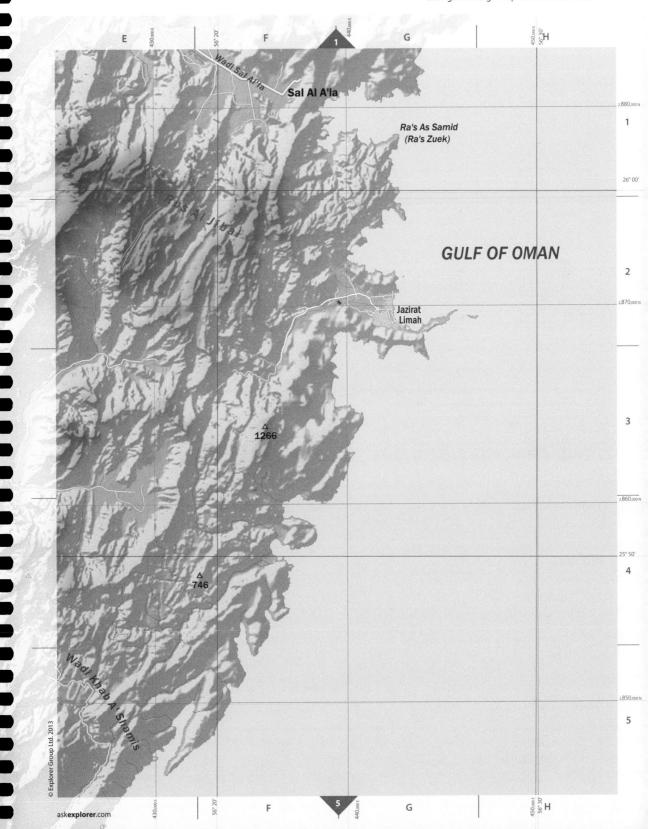

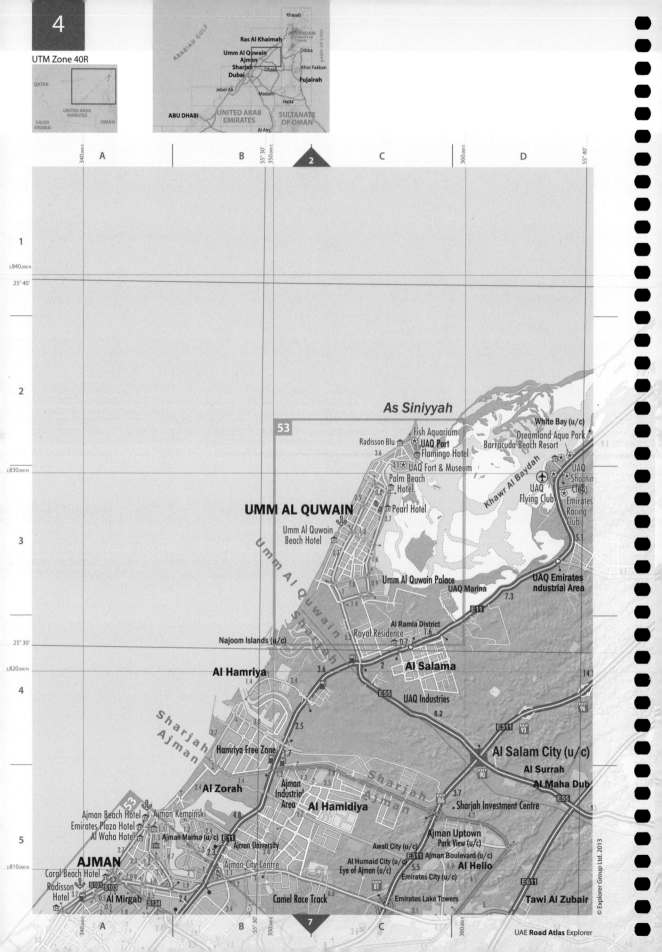

Scale 1: 190,000 1 cm to 1.9 km

N

| 0 | | 10 km |

| 0 | 5 miles |

Each gold UTM grid represents 10km x 10km

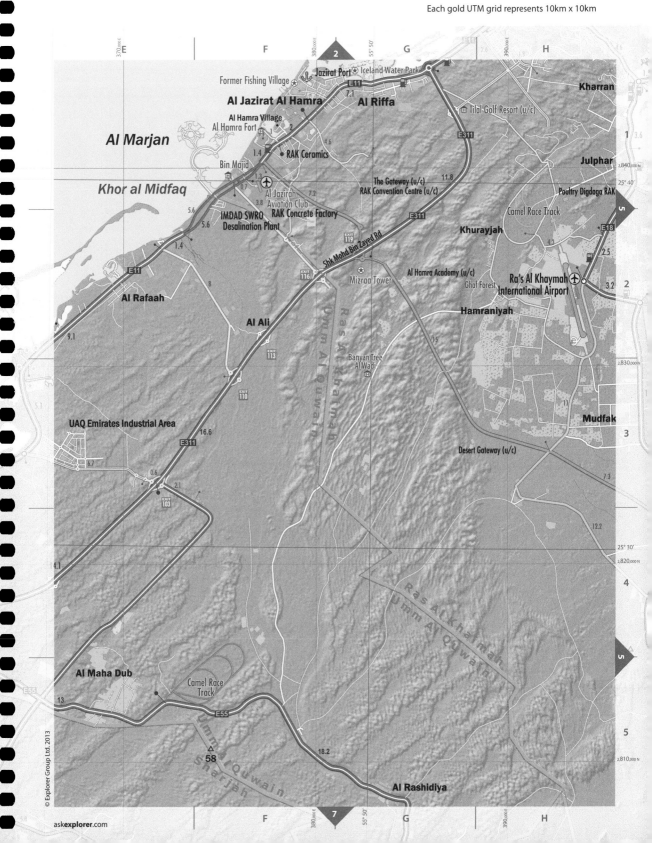

Kharran

E
370,000 E

F

380,000 E

2

55° 50'

G

390,000 E

H

Former Fishing Village

Jazirat Port

Iceland Water Park

Al Jazirat Al Hamra

E11

7.1

Al Riffa

Tilal Golf Resort (u/c)

Al Hamra Village

Al Hamra Fort

1

2

E311

Julphar

2,840,000 N

25° 40'

Al Marjan

RAK Ceramics

4.6

1 3.6

Bin Majid

1.3

Khor al Midfaq

1.4

0.7

Al Jazirah
Aviation Club

3.8

7.2

The Gateway (u/c)
RAK Convention Centre (u/c)

11.8

Poultry Digdaga RAK

Camel Race Track

5.6

IMDAD SWRO
Desalination Plant

RAK Concrete Factory

E311

Khurayjah

5

5.6

EXIT
119

Shk Mohd Bin Zayed Rd

4.3

E18

2.5

1.4

E11

EXIT
116

Al Hamra Academy (u/c)

Ghaf Forest

Ra's Al Khaymah
International Airport

3.2

2

Al Rafaah

Mizraa Tower

Hamraniyah

9.1

Al Ali

EXIT
113

15

Mudfak

3

Banyan Tree
Al Wadi

EXIT
110

5.1

UAQ Emirates Industrial Area

16.6

E311

Desert Gateway (u/c)

7 3

12.2

6.7

0.6

25° 30'

2,820,000 N

2.1

EXIT
103

4

14.1

5

Al Maha Dub

Camel Race
Track

2,810,000 N

E55

13

E55

△
58

18.2

5

Umm Al Quwain Sharjah

Ras Al Khaimah Umm Al Quwain

Al Rashidiya

F

380,000 E

7

55° 50'

G

390,000 E

H

© Explorer Group Ltd. 2013

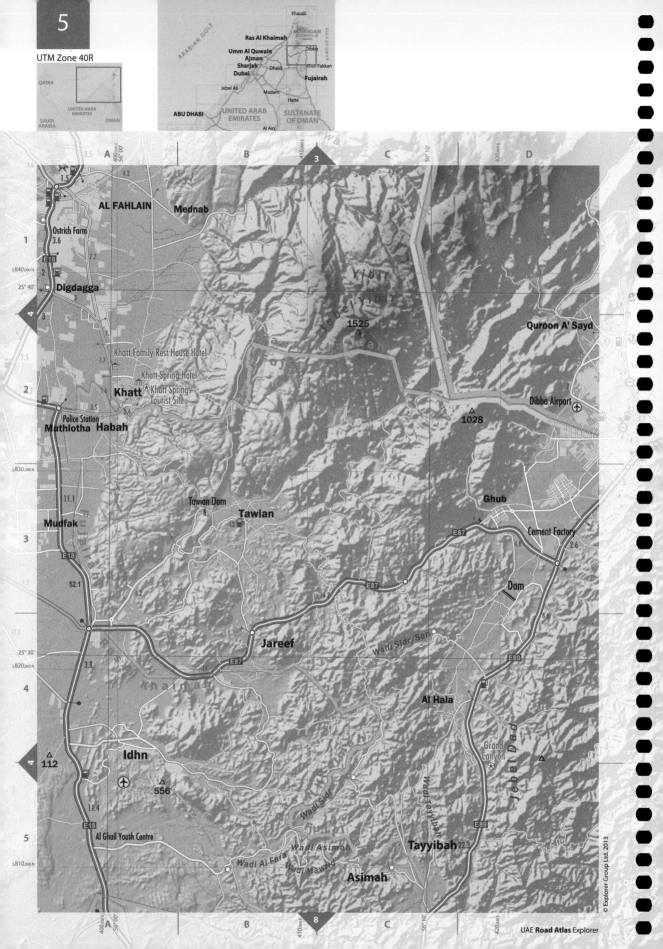

QATAR

UNITED ARAB
EMIRATES

SAUDI
ARABIA   OMAN

ARABIAN GULF

Khasab

MUSANDAM
(SULTANATE OF OMAN)

Ras Al Khaimah
Dibba
Umm Al Quwain
Ajman
Sharjah   Khor Fakkan
Dubai   Dhaid
Fujairah

Jebel Ali   Madam

Hatta

Madam

ABU DHABI   **UNITED ARAB**
EMIRATES   **SULTANATE**
OF OMAN
Al Ain

AL FAHLAIN   **Mednab**

Ostrich Farm
3.6

Digdagga

Khatt Family Rest House Hotel

Khatt Spring Hotel
Khatt ✳ **Khatt Springs**
Tourist Site

Police Station
Mathlotha **Habah**

Mudfak

Tawian Dam
Tawian

Jareef

Wadi Sidr/Sant

Y i b i r

Jebel

1525
△

Quroon A' Sayd

1028
△

Dibba Airport

Ghub
Cement Factory
E87
2.6
E87   Dam
8.6

E89

Al Hala

Grand
Canyon   △

Jebel Dad

△
112

Idhn

△
556

Al Ghail Youth Centre

Wadi Sidr

Wadi Asimah

Wadi Al Fara   Wadi Mawrid

Tayyibah 22.3

Asimah

E89

© Explorer Group Ltd. 2013

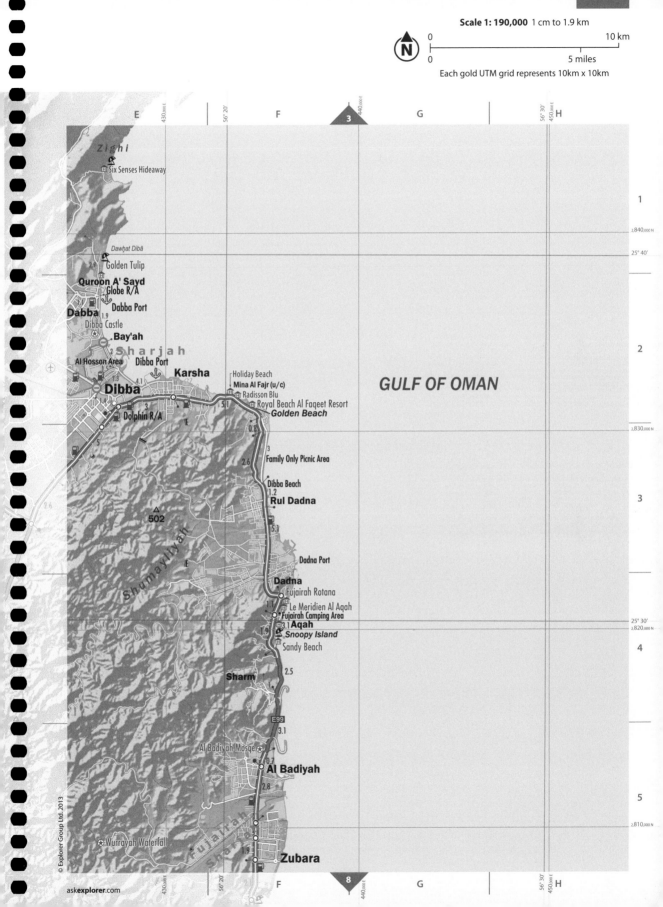

Scale 1: 190,000 1 cm to 1.9 km

0   10 km

0   5 miles

Each gold UTM grid represents 10km x 10km

N

Zighi

Six Senses Hideaway

Dawḥat Dibā

Golden Tulip

Quroon A' Sayd
Globe R/A

Dabba Port

Dabba 1.9

Dibba Castle

Bay'ah

S h a r j a h

Al Hosson Area   Dibba Port

Karsha

Holiday Beach

Dibba

Mina Al Fajr (u/c)

Radisson Blu

Royal Beach Al Faqeet Resort

Golden Beach

Dolphin R/A

0.8

Family Only Picnic Area

2.6

Dibba Beach

Rul Dadna

502

Dadna Port

Shumayliyah

Dadna

Fujairah Rotana

Le Meridien Al Aqah

Fujairah Camping Area

Aqah

Snoopy Island

Sandy Beach

2.5

Sharm

E99

3.1

Al Badiyah Mosque

0.7

Al Badiyah

2.8

GULF OF OMAN

Wurrayah Waterfall

Fujairah

Sharjah

1.9

Zubara

© Explorer Group Ltd. 2013

UTM Zone 40R

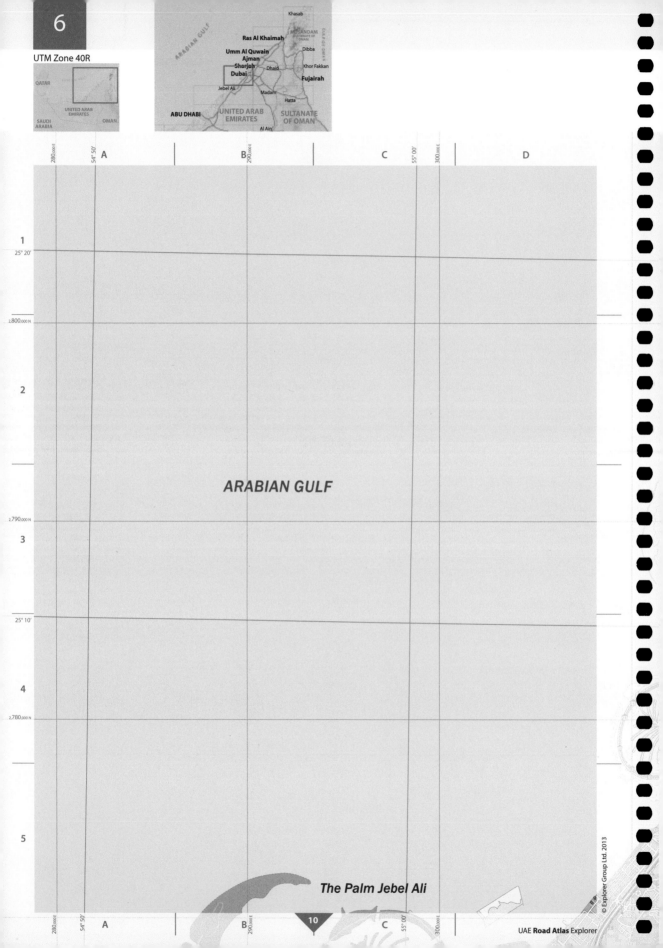

ARABIAN GULF

The Palm Jebel Ali

© Explorer Group Ltd. 2013

Scale 1: 190,000 1 cm to 1.9 km

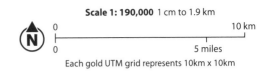

0 ——————————— 10 km

0 ——————————— 5 miles

Each gold UTM grid represents 10km x 10km

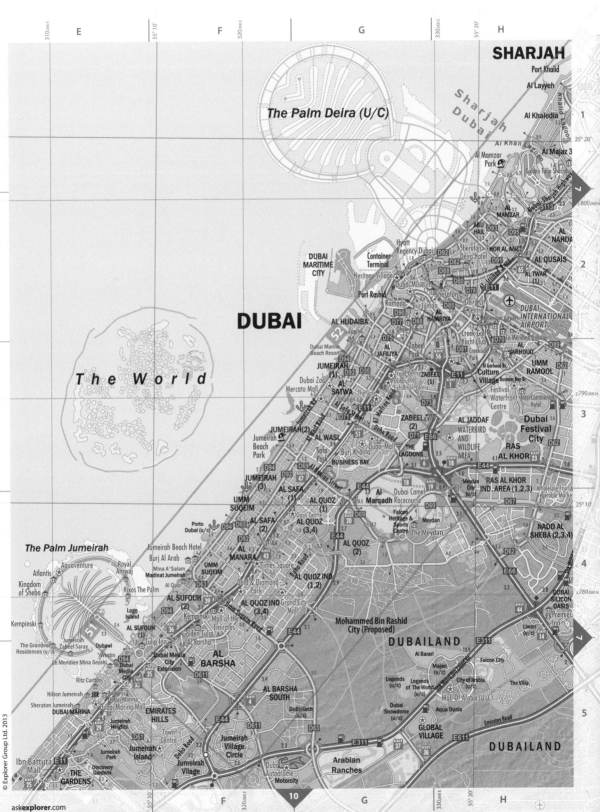

DUBAI

SHARJAH

Port Khalid

Al Layyeh

Al Khaledia

Al Majaz 3

The Palm Deira (U/C)

T h e   W o r l d

The Palm Jumeirah

The Gardens

Ibn Battuta Mall

© Explorer Group Ltd. 2013

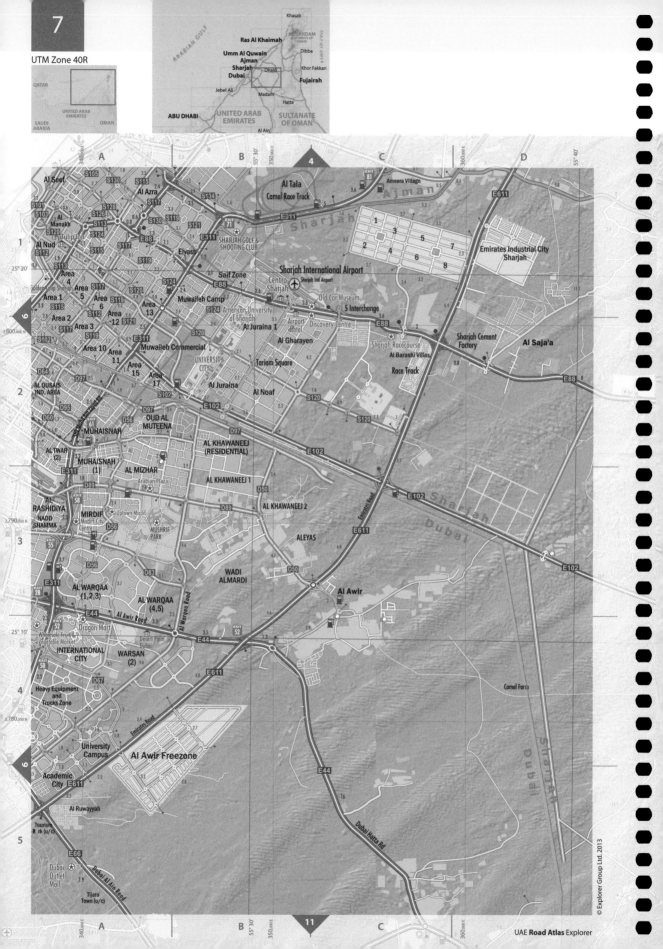

UTM Zone 40R

QATAR
UNITED ARAB
EMIRATES
SAUDI
ARABIA
OMAN

ARABIAN GULF

Khasab
MUSANDAM (SULTANATE OF OMAN)

Ras Al Khaimah
Umm Al Quwain
Ajman
Sharjah
Dubai

Dibba
Khor Fakkan
Fujairah

Jebel Ali
Madam
Hatta

ABU DHABI

UNITED ARAB
EMIRATES

SULTANATE
OF OMAN

Al Ain

4

Al Seef
Al Azra
S105 S130
S115
S134

Al Tala
Camel Race Track
Ameera Village

E611

Ajman

Sharjah

EXIT 81

S101
S103
Al
Manakh
S126 S128
S113
S130
S119
S121

S120
Tulip Inn
Al Nud
S112
S124
S115
E88
S117
S119

EXIT 71
EXIT 7

E311

SHARJAH GOLF &
SHOOTING CLUB

Elyash

1

Emirates Industrial City
Sharjah

Al Saja'a

1
2
3
4
5
6
7
8

Area
4
Golden Tulip Sharjah
Area 1
Area
5
Area
2
Area
6
Area 3
Area 10
Area
11
Area
15
Area
17

S117
S115
S113
S112
S117
S119
S124
S124
S102
D64
D97

Saif Zone
Muwaileh Camp
American University
of Sharjah
Al Juraina 1
Muwaileh Commercial
UNIVERSITY
CITY
Al Juraina
Area
12
Area
13

Sharjah International Airport
Centro
Sharjah
Sharjah Intl Airport
Old Car Museum
5 Interchange
Airport
Hotel
Discovery Centre
Al Gharayen
Tariam Square
Al Noaf

E88
E311
S120
S124
S121
S119
S120

Sharjah Racecourse
Al Barashi Villas
Race Track
E88
S120
S120

Sharjah Cement
Factory

6

AL QUSAIS
IND. AREA
D95
D60
MUHAISNAH
(2)
D56
OUD AL
MUTEENA
AL KHAWANEEJ
(RESIDENTIAL)
E102
D97
E102

D56
AL TWAR
(2)
MUHAISNAH
(1)
AL MIZHAR
Arabian Plaza
AL KHAWANEEJ 1
AL KHAWANEEJ 2

Emirates Road

E611

Sharjah
Dubai

2

AL
RASHIDIYA
NADD
SHAMMA
E311
D89
EXIT 58
MIRDIF
Mirdif City
Centre
MUSHRIF
PARK
Uptown Mirdif
D56
D83
ALEYAS
WADI
ALMARDI
D50

EXIT 55

3

EXIT 28
E311
AL WARQAA
(1,2,3)
AL WARQAA
(4,5)
Al Awir Road
D50
Al Awir
E611

E44
EXIT 52
EXIT 52
Dragon Mart
Wholesale Fruit &
Vegetable Market
INTERNATIONAL
CITY
WARSAN
(2)
Desert Palm
Dubai
E44
EXIT 30
D67

Al Warqaa Road

4

Heavy Equipment
and
Trucks Zone
E611
Camel Farm

University
Campus

Emirates Road

6

Academic
City
E611
Al Ruwayyah
Tourism
Park (u/c)
Al Awir Freezone
E44

Dubai
Outlet
Mall
Tijara
Town (u/c)
E66
Dubai Al Ain Road
Dubai Hatta Rd

5

© Explorer Group Ltd. 2013

A   B   11   C   D

Scale 1: 190,000 1 cm to 1.9 km

0   10 km

0   5 miles

Each gold UTM grid represents 10km x 10km

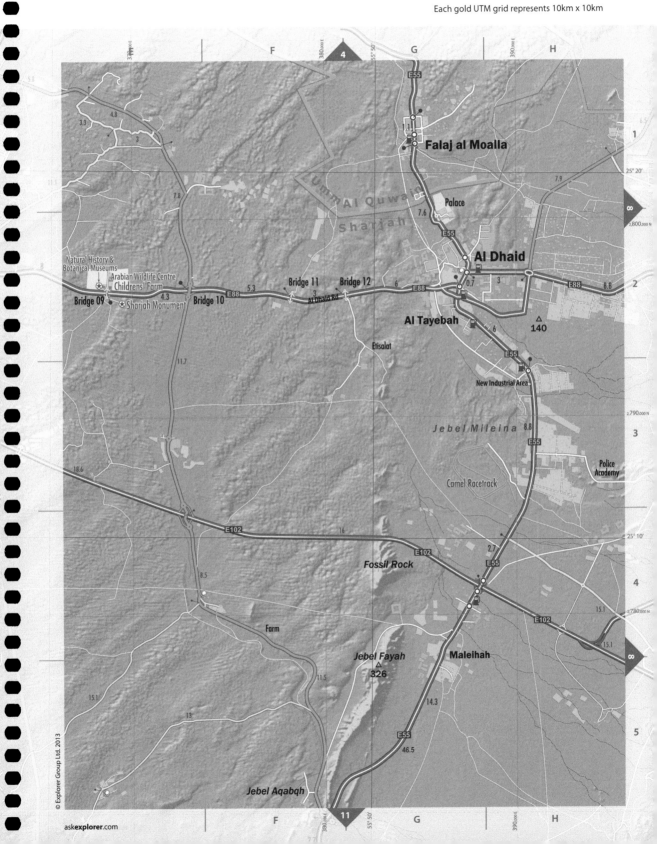

UTM Zone 40R

QATAR

UNITED ARAB
EMIRATES

SAUDI
ARABIA

OMAN

ARABIAN GULF

Khasab

MUSANDAM
(CLIMATE OF OMAN)

Ras Al Khaimah

Dibba

Umm Al Quwain
Ajman
Sharjah
Dubai

Dhaid

Khor Fakkan

Fujairah

Jebel Ali

Madam

Hatta

ABU DHABI

UNITED ARAB
EMIRATES

SULTANATE
OF OMAN

Al Ain

A 5 **B** **C** **D**

△ 723

E89

1

25° 20'

Manama

Masafi Town

Masafi
Al Boom
Tourist Village

Mineral Springs

Masafi

Shis

2,800,000 N

Sharjah
Ajman

E18

E88

16.8

E88

Friday Market

Wadi Shis Pool

Waterfall

Jebel Al HTiqah

2

E88

Poultry Farm

Dam

E88

Wadi Daftah

Wadi Siji

267 △

2,790,000 N

3

Maghribiyah

11.3

Wadi Farfar

△ 725

Wadi Ham

E89

25° 10'

Sifuni

20

4

Ras Al Khaimah

11

1,780,000 N

259 △ Dam

Al Khari

3.4

△ 1034

5

Shawka

Fort Hayl

E102

Wadi Hay

Sharjah

E102

A 12 **B** **C** **D**

© Explorer Group Ltd. 2013

UAE Road Atlas Explorer

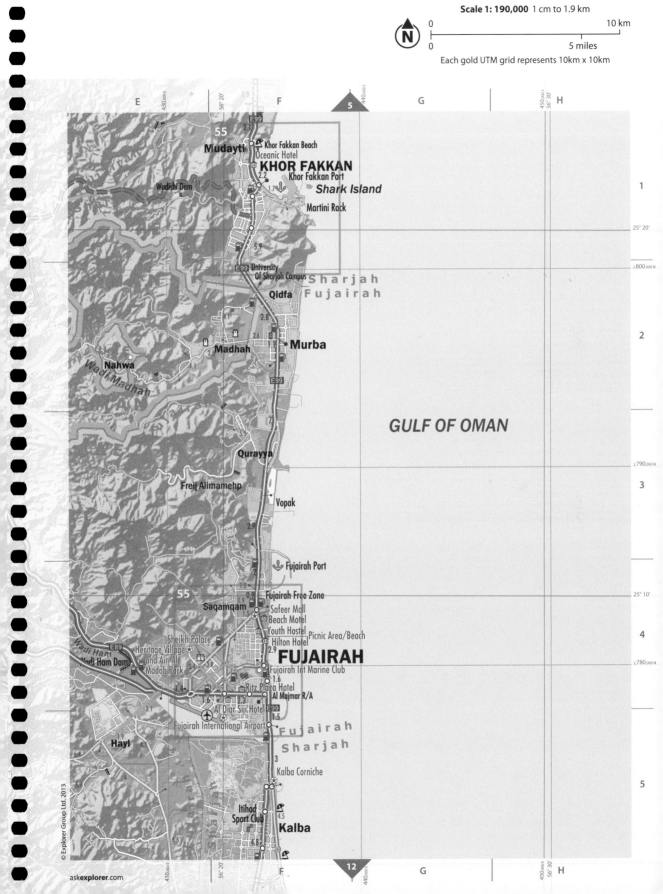

N

E   430,000 E   56° 20'   1.9   F   440,000 E   **5**   G   450,000 E 56° 30'   H

55

E99

2.1

Khor Fakkan Beach

Mudayti

Oceanic Hotel

KHOR FAKKAN

2.2

Khor Fakkan Port

Shark Island

1.7

Wadishi Dam

Martini Rock

1

25° 20'

2,800,000 N

5.9

E99 University

Of Sharjah Campus

Sharjah

Fujairah

Qidfa

1.1

2.8

2.6

1.1   **Murba**

Madhah

2

2.7

4.1

Nahwa

Wadi Madhah

E99

O M A N

7

GULF OF OMAN

5.5

Qurayya

2,790,000 N

Freij Alimamehp

3

Vopak

2.9

Fujairah Port

1.2

55

0.8

Fujairah Free Zone

1.9

Saqamqam

Safeer Mall

Beach Motel

25° 10'

Youth Hostel   Picnic Area/Beach

Sheikh Palace

Hilton Hotel

4

Heritage Village

2,780,000 N

Wadi Ham

E89   and Ain Al

Wadi Ham Dam

Madab Park

3.3

FUJAIRAH

Fujairah Int Marine Club

1.6

1.4

Ritz Plaza Hotel

1.6

2.3

Al Majmar R/A

2.1

Al Diar Siji Hotel

E99

1.5

Fujairah International Airport

Fujairah

1.9

Sharjah

Hayl

4.1

3

Kalba Corniche

5

Itihad

Sport Club

4.5

6.5   4.8   **Kalba**

UTM Zone 40R

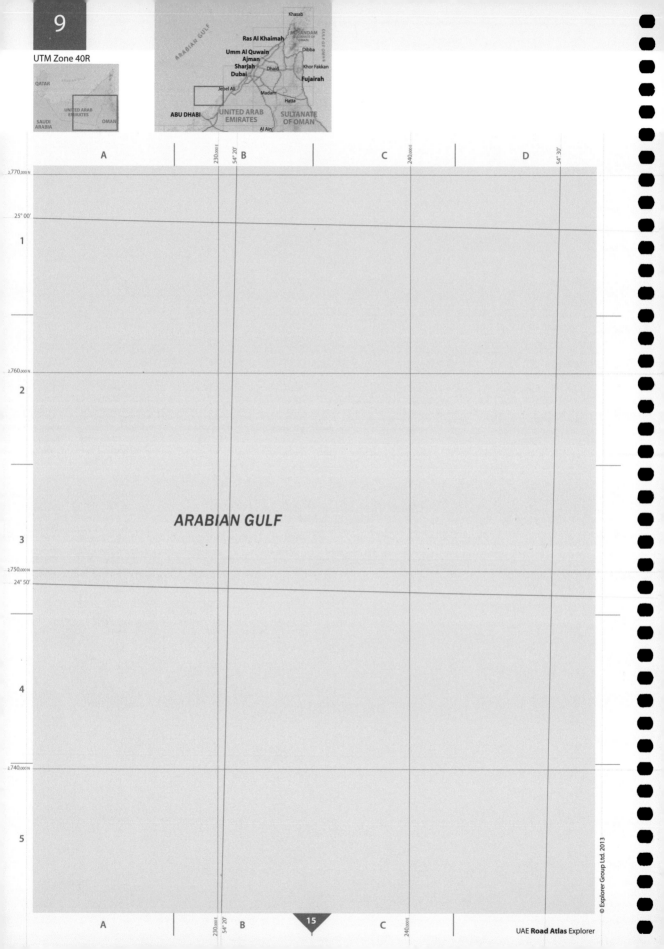

ARABIAN GULF

© Explorer Group Ltd. 2013

Scale 1: 190,000 1 cm to 1.9 km

N

| 0 | 10 km |
| 0 | 5 miles |

Each gold UTM grid represents 10km x 10km

E   F   G   H

1   25° 00'

ARABIAN GULF

10

2

3   24° 50'

Ghantoot
Lagoon

Ras Ghantoot   Ghantoot
Lagoon

Emirates Aluminium (EMAL)
Smelter Complex Project

Khalifa Port & Industrial
Zone (KPIZ) (u/c)

Al Taweelah Power &
Desalination Complex

Sabkhat al' Aysh   4

10

Al Taweelah

Ras Ghanadah

Ras Sadr   UAE Naval College   SabBirkat Sumayh   Al Samha

New Port City   Samha

5

E11

EXIT
381

15   F   G   H

© Explorer Group Ltd. 2013

askexplorer.com

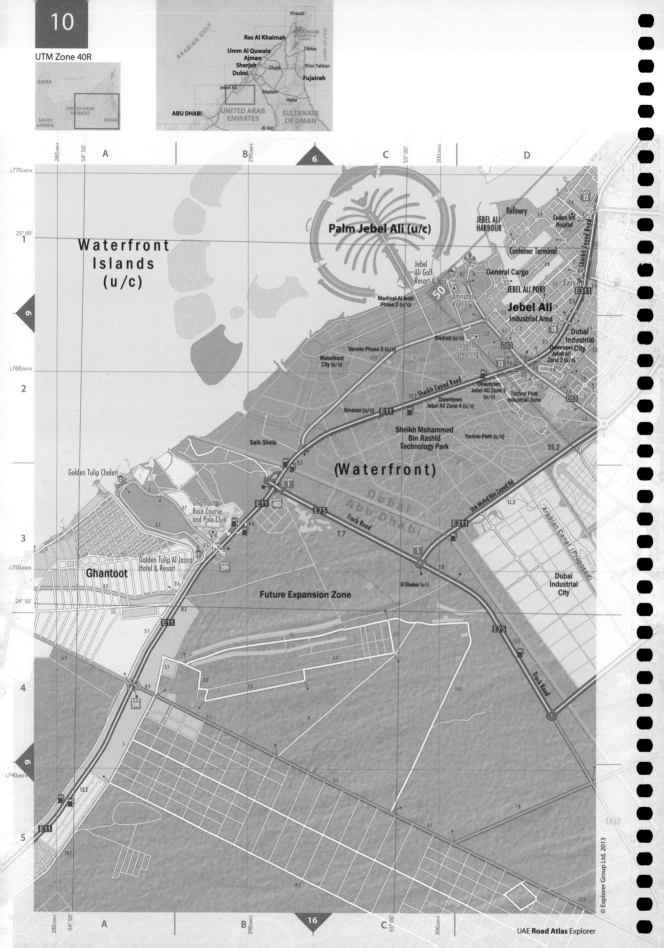

UTM Zone 40R

Ras Al Khaimah
Umm Al Quwain
Ajman
Sharjah
Dubai
ABU DHABI
UNITED ARAB
EMIRATES
SULTANATE
OF OMAN
Khasab
Dibba
Khor Fakkan
Fujairah
Jebel Ali
Madam
Hatta
Al Ain
Dhaid

6

Waterfront
Islands
(u/c)

Palm Jebel Ali (u/c)

JEBEL ALI
HARBOUR

Refinery

Cedars Int'l
Hospital

EXIT 22

Container Terminal

General Cargo

JEBEL ALI PORT

Jebel Ali Golf
Resort & Spa

Madinat Al Arab
Phase 2 (u/c)

Emirates
Kart Club

50

Jebel Ali
Industrial Area

EXIT 18

Dubai
Industrial
City

Badrah (u/c)

Jebel Ali
Shooting Club

D53

Downtown
Jebel Ali
Zone 2 (u/c)

Veneto Phase 3 (u/c)

Waterfront
City (u/c)

Downtown
Jebel Ali Zone 3
(u/c)

EXIT 13

Sheikh Zayed Road

Omaran (u/c)

E11

Downtown
Jebel Ali Zone 4 (u/c)

Techno Park
Industrial Zone

D53

Saih Sheib

Sheikh Mohammed
Bin Rashid
Technology Park

Techno Park (u/c)

35.2

(Waterfront)

Golden Tulip Chalets

Ghantoot
Race Course
and Polo Club

EXIT 1

E11

EXIT 403

E75

Dubai
Abu Dhabi

Truck Road

Shk Mohd Bin Zayed Rd

E311

Arabian Canal (Proposed)

EXIT 399

Golden Tulip Al Jazira
Hotel & Resort

7.7

EXIT

Ghantoot

Future Expansion Zone

Al Ghadeer (u/c)

1.8

Dubai
Industrial
City

E11

EXIT 390

E75

E75

Truck Road

13.2

E75

E11

UAE Road Atlas Explorer

© Explorer Group Ltd. 2013

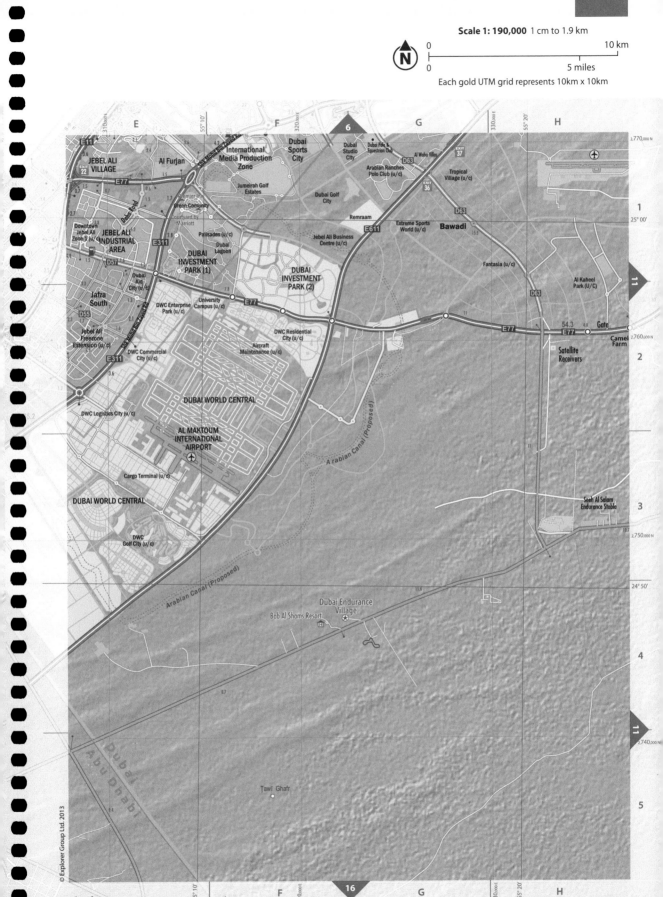

© Explorer Group Ltd. 2013

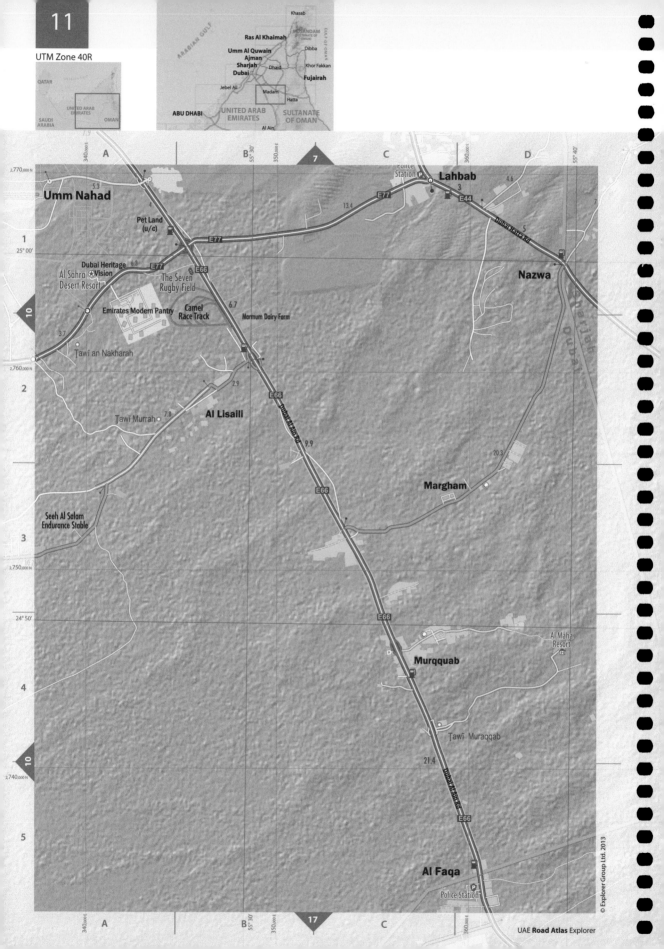

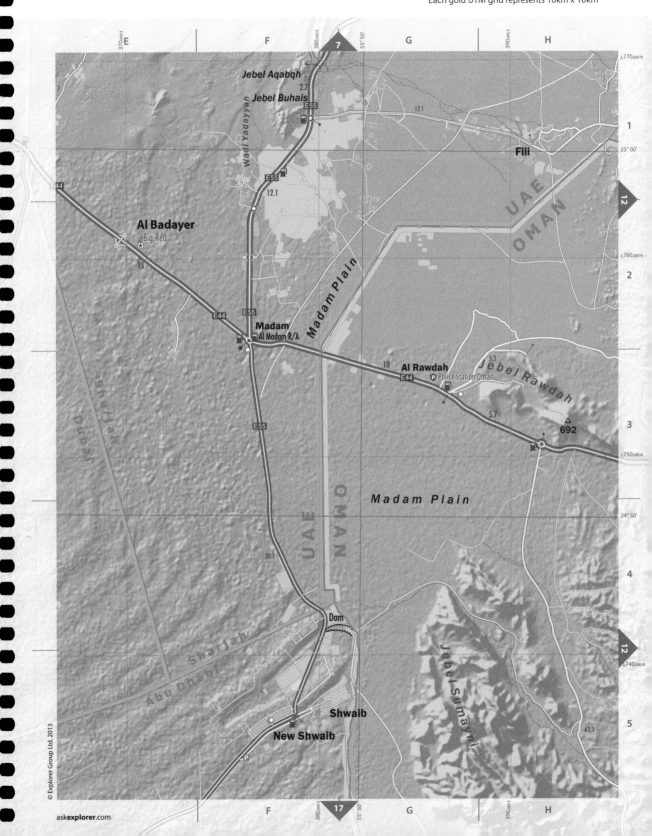

Scale 1: 190,000 1 cm to 1.9 km

0   10 km

0   5 miles

Each gold UTM grid represents 10km x 10km

Jebel Aqabqh

Jebel Buhais

Wadi Yadayyah

Fili

UAE

OMAN

Al Badayer
Big Red

Madam Plain

Madam
Al Madam R/A

Al Rawdah
Police Station Oman

Jebel Rawdah

△ 692

UAE

OMAN

Madam Plain

Sharjah

Dubai

Sharjah

Abu Dhabi

Dam

Jebel Sumayni

Shwaib

New Shwaib

UTM Zone 40R

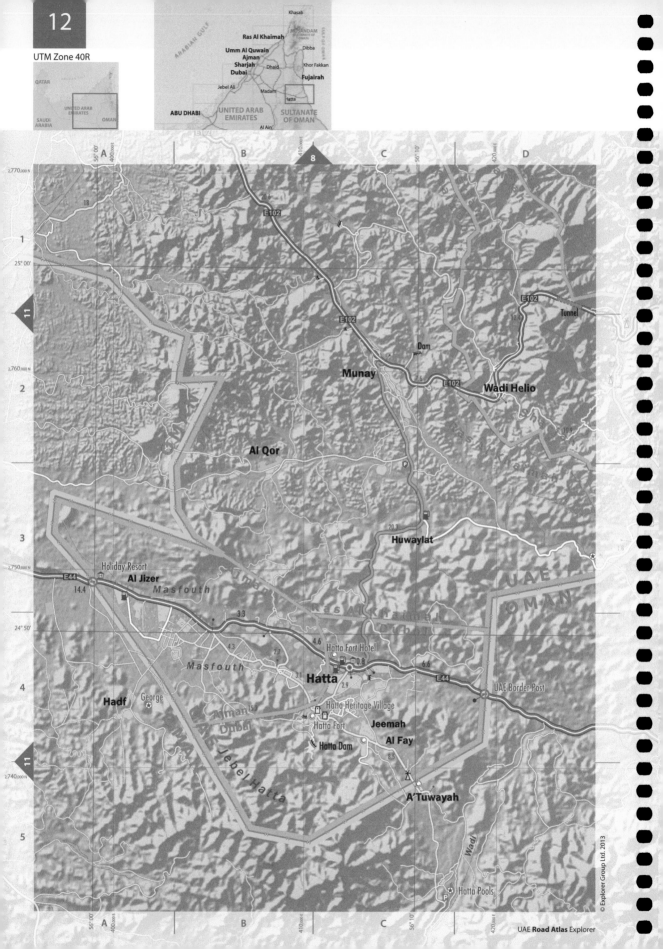

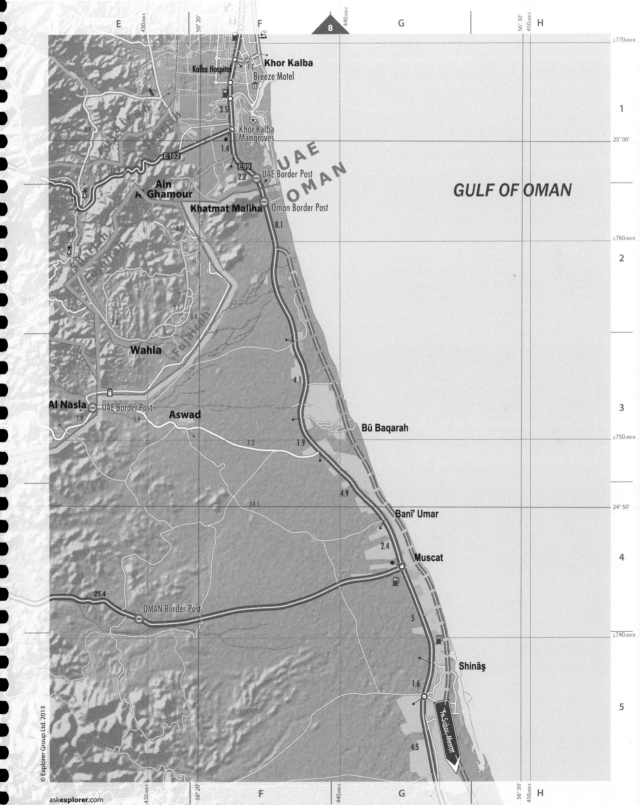

GULF OF OMAN

Khor Kalba
Kalba Hospital
Breeze Motel
Khor Kalba Mangroves
E102
Ain A' Ghamour
E99
UAE Border Post
Khatmat Maliha   Oman Border Post
UAE
OMAN
Wahla
Al Nasla   UAE Border Post
Aswad
Bū Baqarah
Banī' Umar
Muscat
OMAN Border Post
Shināṣ
To Saham-Muscat

Each gold UTM grid represents 10km x 10km

UTM Zone 39R

QATAR

ABU DHABI

Sila · Jebel Dhana

Madinat Zayed

UNITED ARAB EMIRATES

SAUDI ARABIA

Mazaira

QATAR

UNITED ARAB EMIRATES

SAUDI ARABIA

OMAN

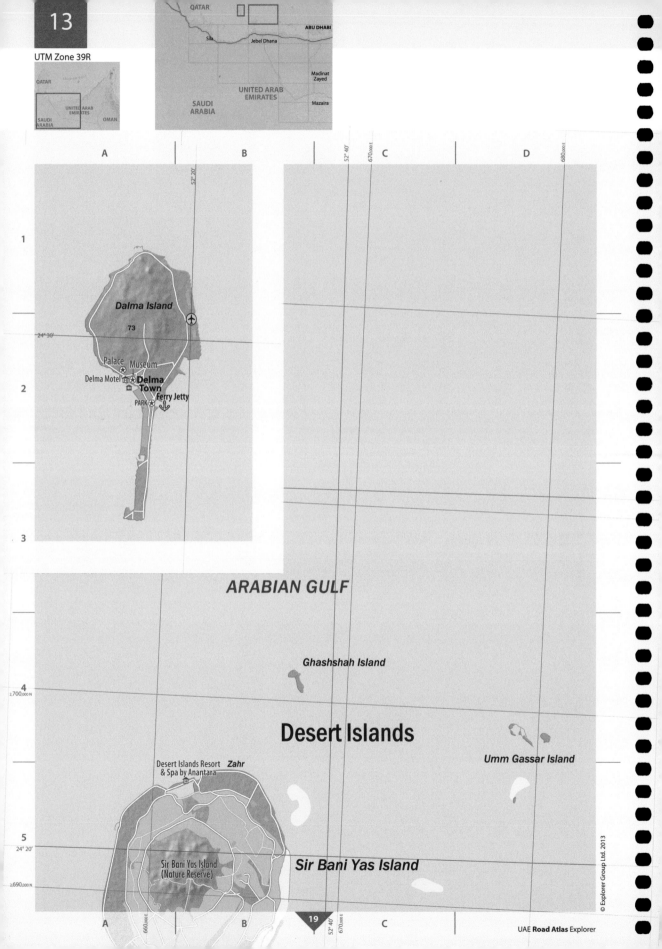

	A	B	C	D

52° 20'

52° 40'   670,000 E

680,000 E

1

Dalma Island

73

Palace   Museum

Delma Motel   **Delma Town**

24° 30'

PARK   Ferry Jetty

2

3

ARABIAN GULF

Ghashshah Island

4

2,700,000 N

Desert Islands

Umm Gassar Island

Desert Islands Resort & Spa by Anantara   *Zahr*

5

24° 20'

Sir Bani Yas Island (Nature Reserve)

Sir Bani Yas Island

2,690,000 N

A	B	C

660,000 E

52° 40'

670,000 E

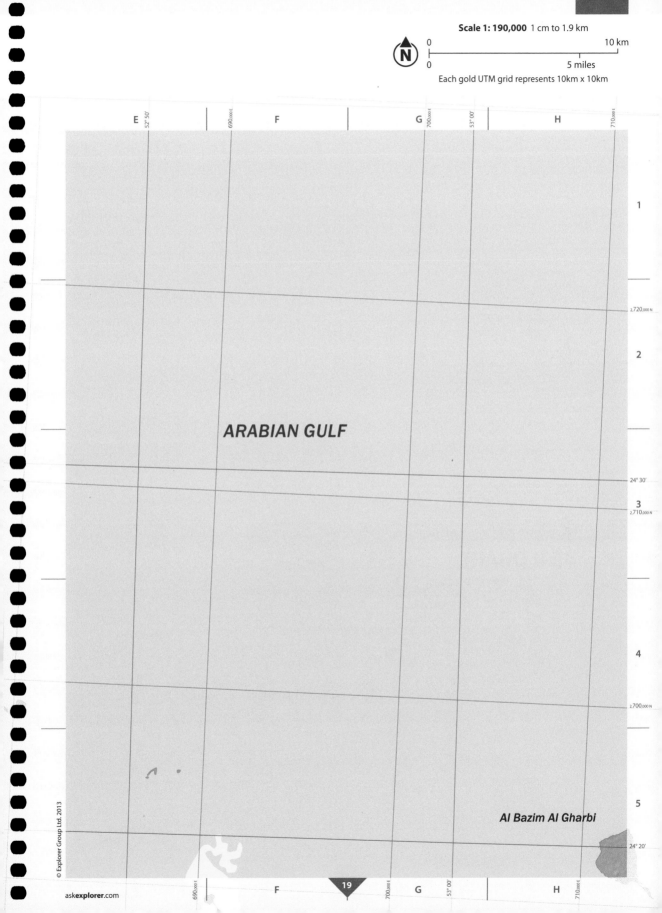

ARABIAN GULF

Al Bazim Al Gharbi

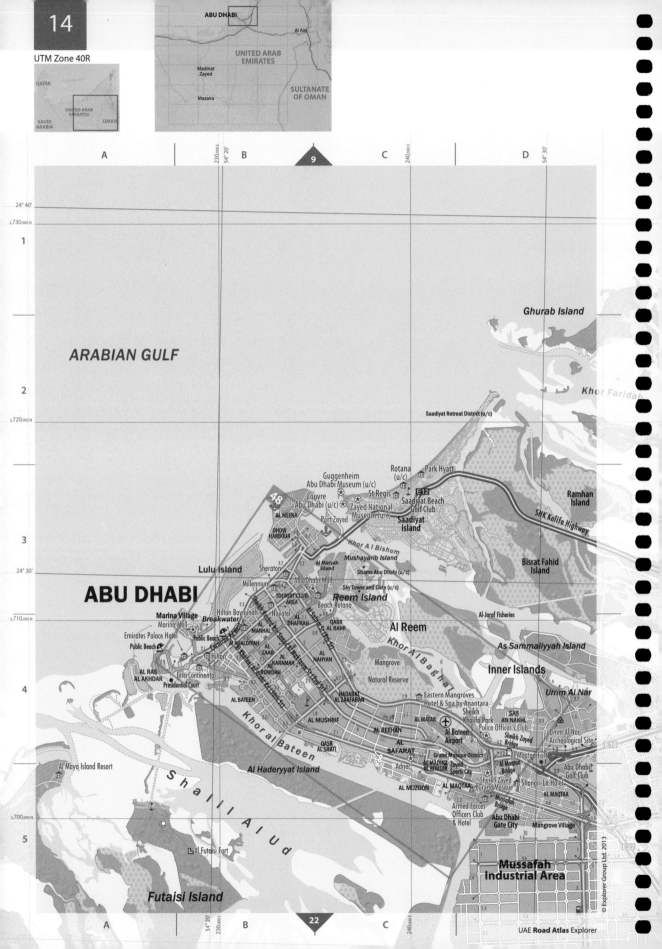

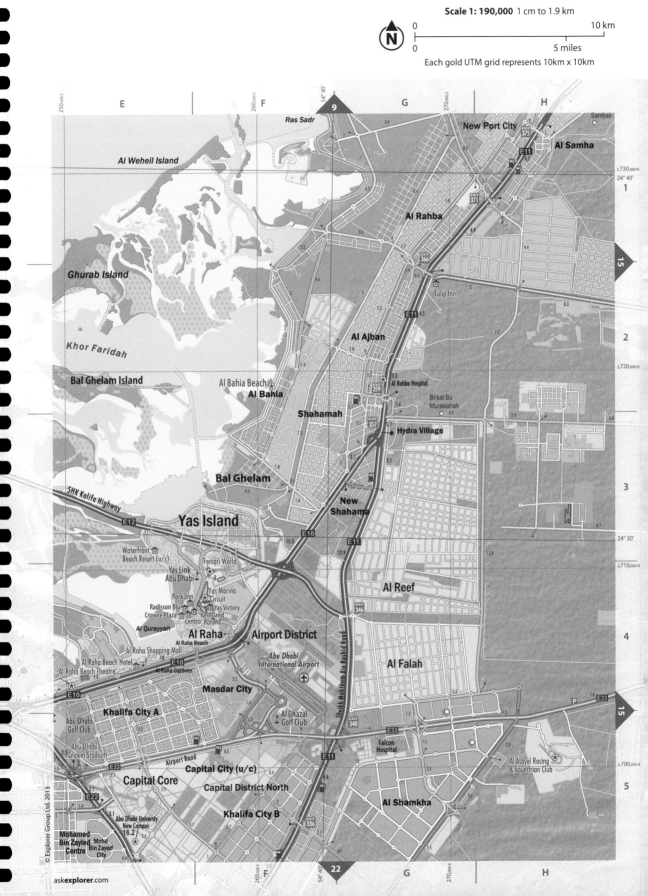

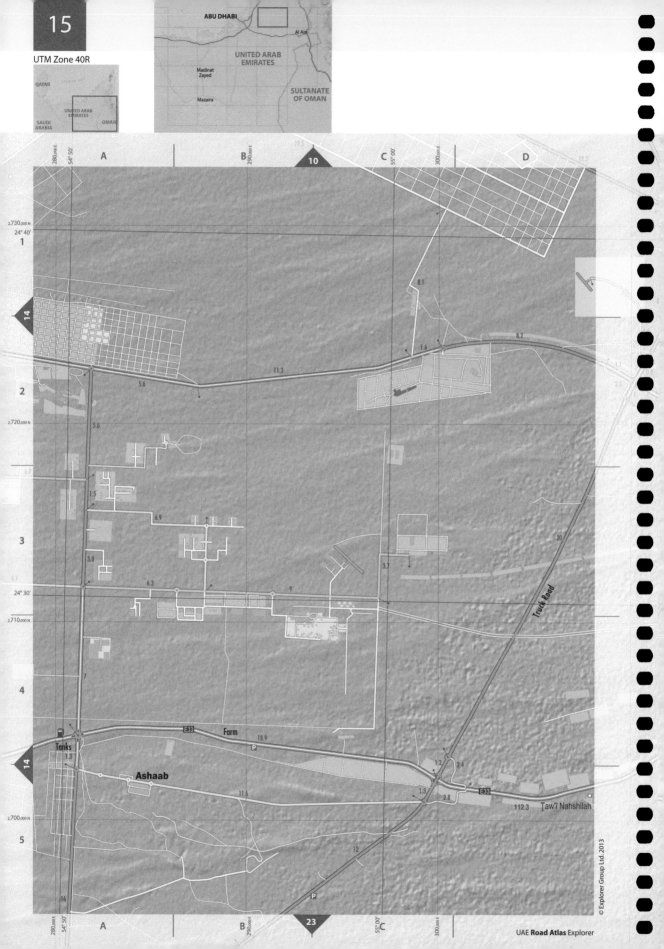

Scale 1: 190,000 1 cm to 1.9 km

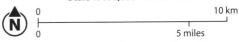

0   10 km

0   5 miles

Each gold UTM grid represents 10km x 10km

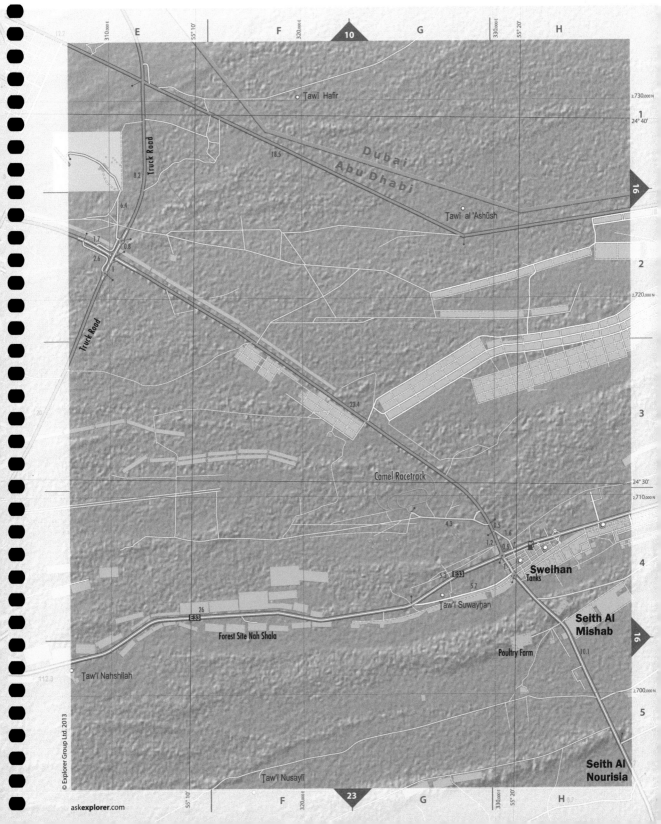

UTM Zone 40R

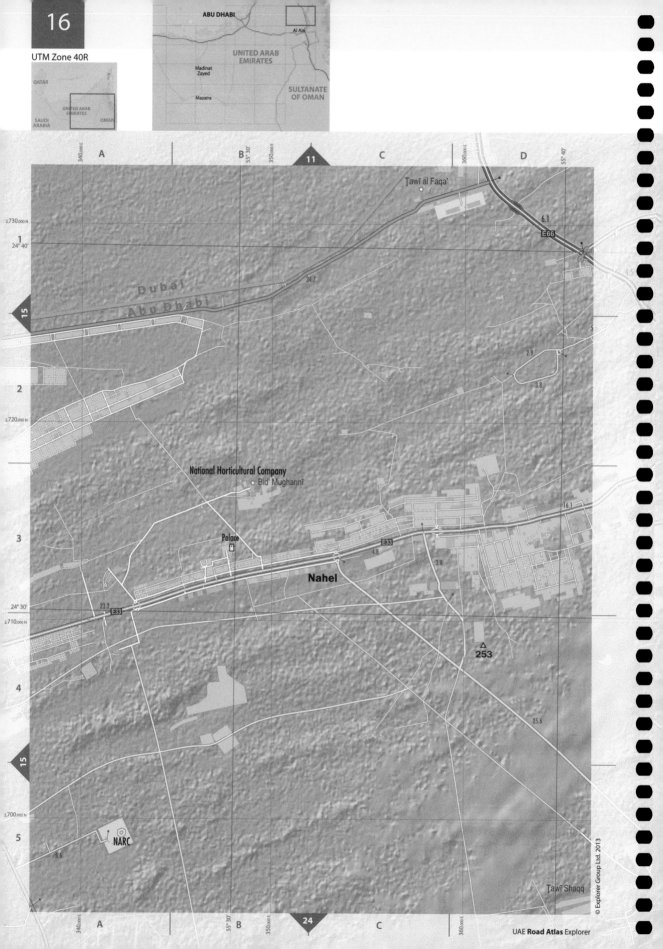

ABU DHABI

Al Ain

UNITED ARAB
EMIRATES

Madinat
Zayed

Mazaira

SULTANATE
OF OMAN

QATAR

UNITED ARAB
EMIRATES

SAUDI
ARABIA   OMAN

A   **B**   55° 30'   **11**   **C**   **D**   55° 40'

Ṭawī al Faqa'

6.1

E66

2,730,000 N

1
24° 40'

Dubai
Abu Dhabi

34.7

2.9

3.8

2

2,720,000 N

National Horticultural Company
○ Bid' Mughannī

Palace

3

E33

4.8

3.8

16.1

Nahel

24° 30'

23.2

E33

2,710,000 N

△
253

4

25.6

15

2,700,000 N

5

⊡
NARC

9.6

Ṭawī Shaqq

A   55° 30'   **B**   350,000 E   **24**   **C**   360,000 E

Scale 1: 190,000 1 cm to 1.9 km

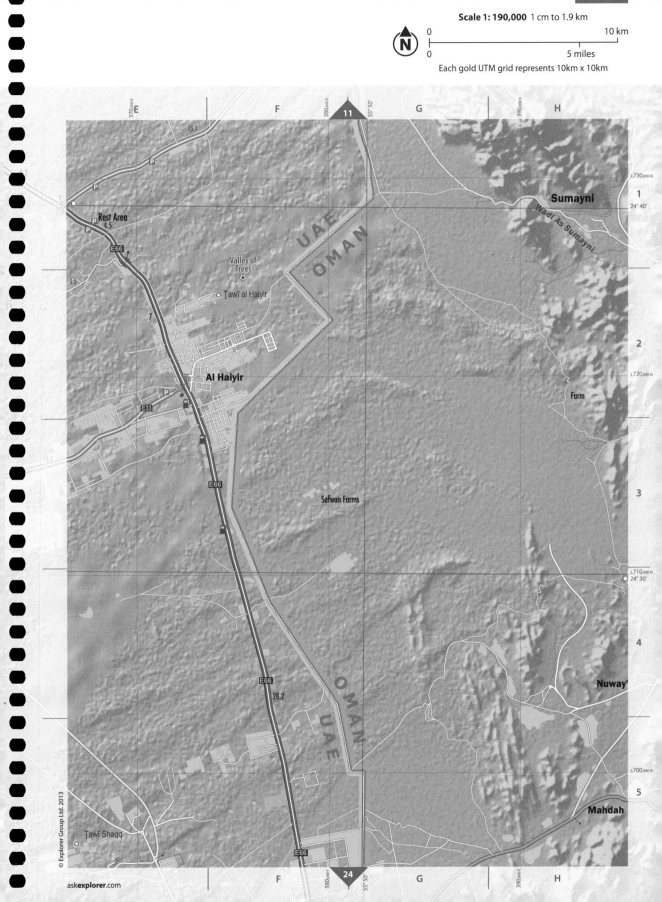

0   10 km

0   5 miles

Each gold UTM grid represents 10km x 10km

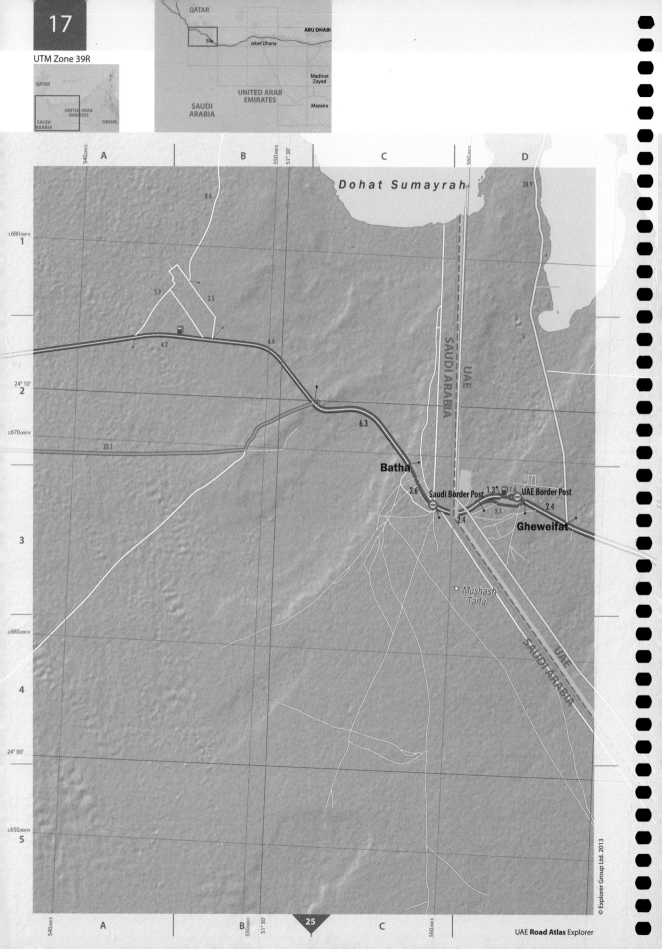

UTM Zone 39R

QATAR
ABU DHABI
Sila
Jebel Dhana
UNITED ARAB
EMIRATES
Madinat
Zayed
SAUDI
ARABIA
Mazaira

QATAR
UNITED ARAB
EMIRATES
SAUDI
ARABIA
OMAN

Dohat Sumayrah

A   B   C   D

2,680,000 N
1

8.6

28.9

5.9   3.5

4.2   6.6

11.2

24° 10'
2

22.1

6.3

2,670,000 N

Batha

2.6

Saudi Border Post   1.3   1.6   UAE Border Post

2.4   2.7   2.4

Gheweifat

3

2,660,000 N

Mushash
Tarfa

4

24° 00'

2,650,000 N
5

© Explorer Group Ltd. 2013

SAUDI ARABIA
UAE

UAE
SAUDI ARABIA

540,000 E
550,000 E
51° 30'
560,000 E

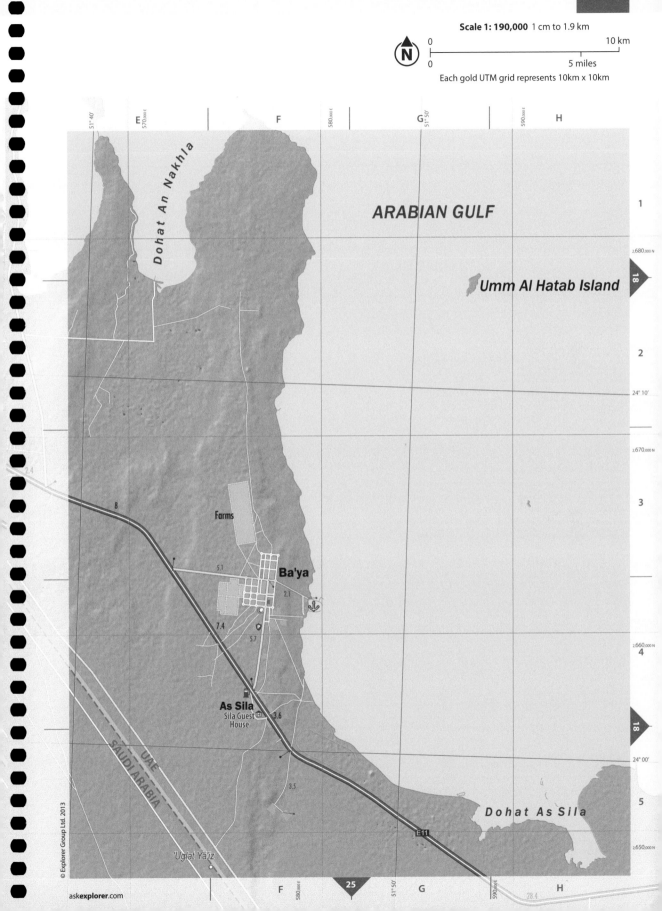

Scale 1 : 190,000 1 cm to 1.9 km

N

0   10 km

0   5 miles

Each gold UTM grid represents 10km x 10km

ARABIAN GULF

Umm Al Hatab Island

Dohat An Nakhla

Farms

Ba'ya

As Sila
Sila Guest
House

UAE
SAUDI ARABIA

Dohat As Sila

'Uglat Ya'iz

E11

© Explorer Group Ltd 2013

askexplorer.com

UTM Zone 39R

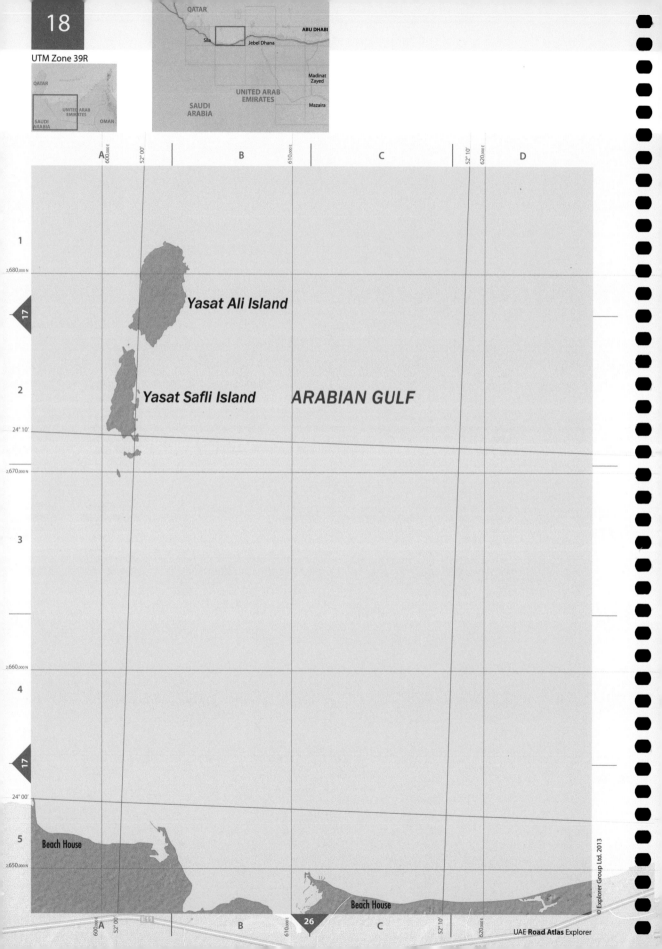

QATAR

Sila Jebel Dhana

ABU DHABI

Madinat Zayed

UNITED ARAB EMIRATES

SAUDI ARABIA

Mazaira

Yasat Ali Island

Yasat Safli Island

ARABIAN GULF

Beach House

Beach House

E11

26

© Explorer Group Ltd. 2013

Scale 1: 190,000 1 cm to 1.9 km

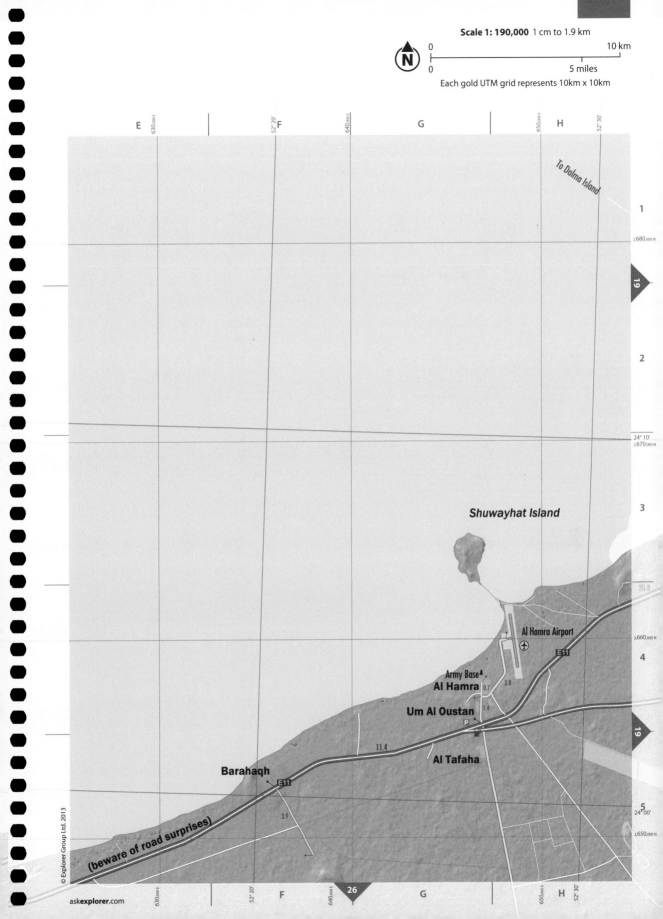

Each gold UTM grid represents 10km x 10km

0 — 10 km

0 — 5 miles

To Dalma Island

Shuwayhat Island

20.8

Al Hamra Airport

E11

Army Base
Al Hamra 0.7   3.8

1.4

Um Al Oustan

P

11.4

Al Tafaha

Barahaqh

E11

3.9

(beware of road surprises)

© Explorer Group Ltd. 2013

E 630,000 E 52° 20' F 640,000 E G 650,000 E H 52° 30'

2,680,000 N

24° 10' 2,670,000 N

2,660,000 N

24° 00' 2,650,000 N

1 2 3 4 5

19 19

26

UTM Zone 39R

QATAR

ABU DHABI

Jebel Dhana

Sila

Madinat
Zayed

UNITED ARAB
EMIRATES

SAUDI
ARABIA

Mazaira

QATAR

UNITED ARAB
EMIRATES

SAUDI
ARABIA

OMAN

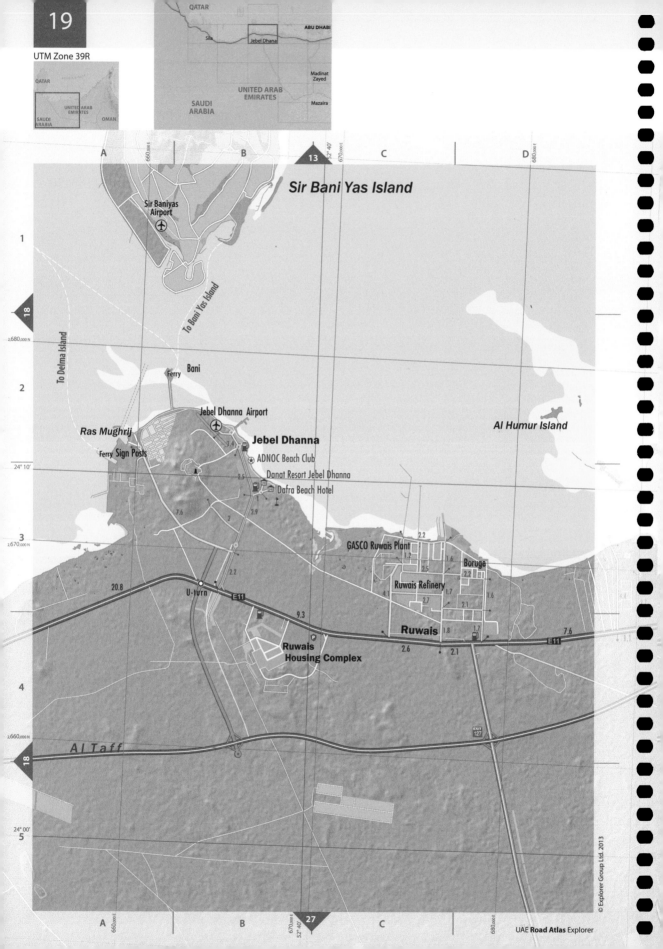

13

A   660,000 E   B   52° 40'   670,000 E   C   680,000 E   D

Sir Bani Yas Island

Sir Baniyas
Airport

1

18

2,680,000 N

To Delma Island

To Bani Yas Island

Ferry   Bani

2

Ras Mughrij

Jebel Dhanna Airport

Al Humur Island

Ferry Sign Posts

Jebel Dhanna

1.4

ADNOC Beach Club

24° 10'

9.5

Danat Resort Jebel Dhanna

Dafra Beach Hotel

7.6

2

2.9

3

2,670,000 N

GASCO Ruwais Plant

2.2

1.2

2.5

Boruge

2.2

Ruwais Refinery

1.7

1.6

2.2

4.1

2.7

2.1

20.8

U-turn

E11

9.3

1.8

1.7

Ruwais

7.6

E11

2.6

2.1

1.1

4

P

**Ruwais
Housing Complex**

2,660,000 N

Al Taff

EXIT
127

18

24° 00'

5

© Explorer Group Ltd. 2013

A   660,000 E   B   670,000 E   52° 40'   C   680,000 E

27

UAE **Road Atlas** Explorer

Scale 1: 190,000 1 cm to 1.9 km

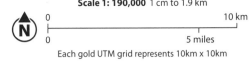

Each gold UTM grid represents 10km x 10km

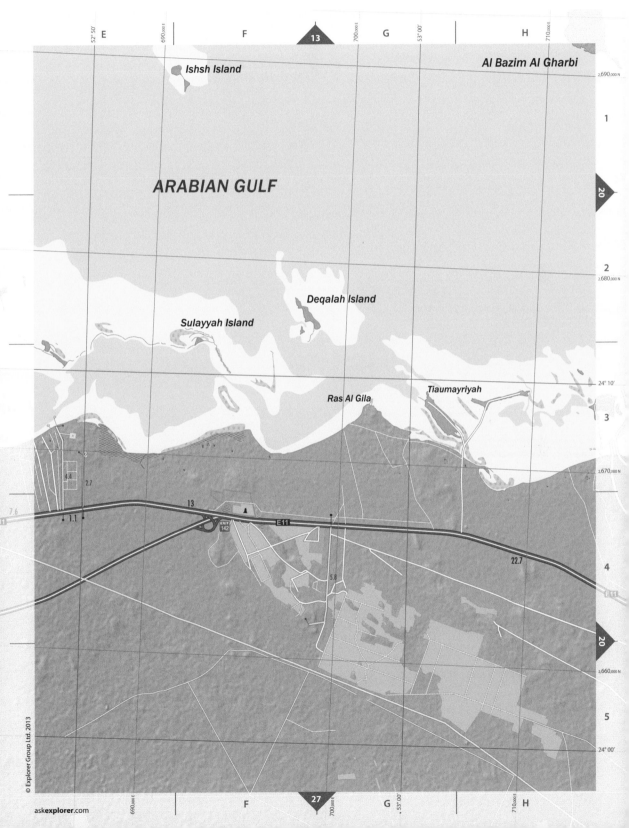

Ishsh Island

Al Bazim Al Gharbi

ARABIAN GULF

Deqalah Island

Sulayyah Island

Ras Al Gila

Tiaumayriyah

E11

13

EXIT
142

E11

22.7

E11

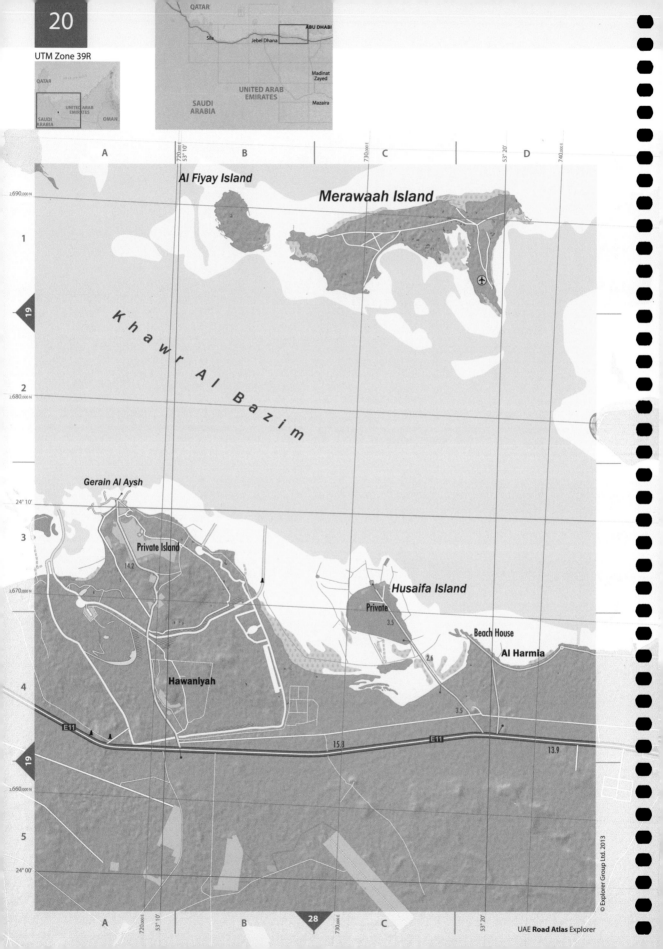

UTM Zone 39R

QATAR
ABU DHABI
Sila   Jebel Dhana
Madinat
Zayed
UNITED ARAB
EMIRATES
SAUDI
ARABIA   Mazaira

QATAR
UNITED ARAB
EMIRATES
SAUDI
ARABIA   OMAN

Al Fiyay Island

Merawaah Island

Khawr Al Bazim

Gerain Al Aysh

Private Island

14.2

Husaifa Island

Private

3.5

Beach House

Al Harmia

2.6

Hawaniyah

E11

E11

15.8

3.5

13.9

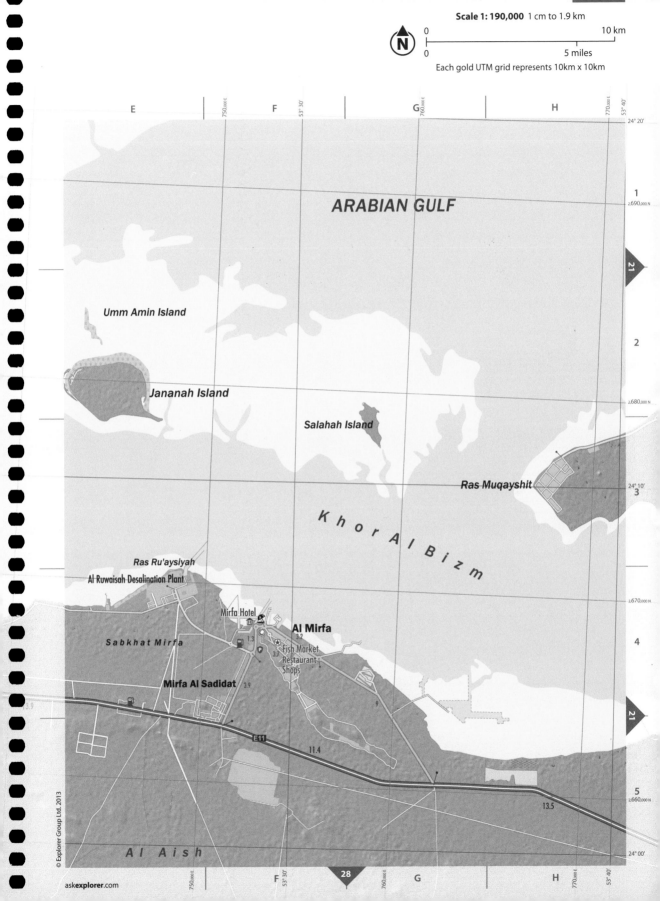

Scale 1: 190,000 1 cm to 1.9 km

0   10 km

0   5 miles

Each gold UTM grid represents 10km x 10km

E   750,000 E   F   53° 30'   G   760,000 E   H   770,000 E   53° 40'

24° 20'

ARABIAN GULF

1

2,690,000 N

21

Umm Amin Island

2

Jananah Island

2,680,000 N

Salahah Island

K h o r   A l   B i z m

24° 10'

Ras Muqayshit

3

Ras Ru'aysiyah

Al Ruwaisah Desalination Plant

2,670,000 N

Mirfa Hotel

Al Mirfa
3.2

Sabkhat Mirfa   1.3

Fish Market
Restaurant
Shops

4

21

Mirfa Al Sadidat   3.9

9

3.9

E11   11.4

5

13.5

2,660,000 N

A l   A i s h

24° 00'

750,000 E   F   53° 30'   760,000 E   G   H   770,000 E   53° 40'

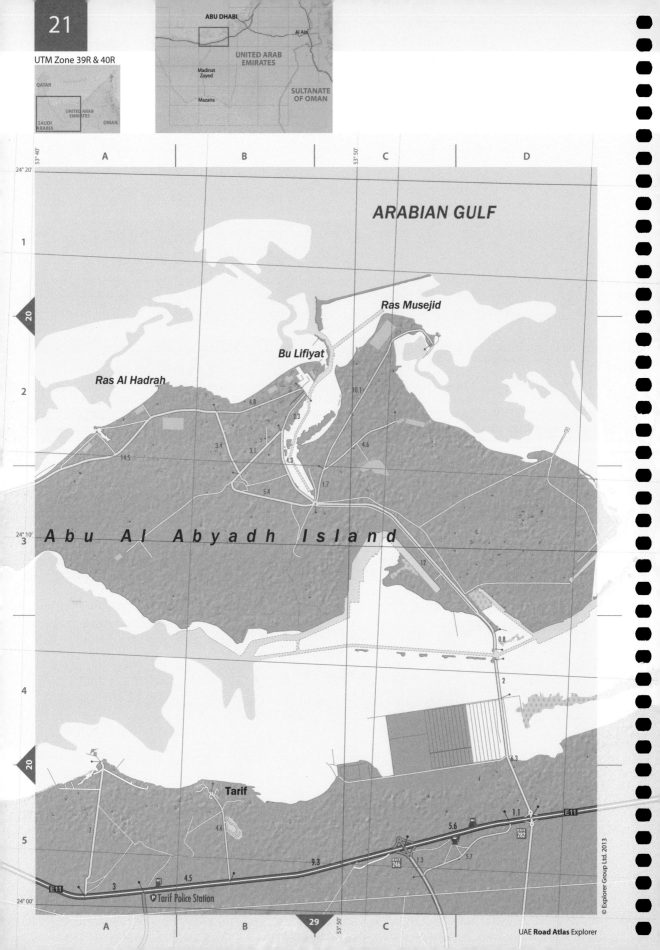

UTM Zone 39R & 40R

QATAR

UNITED ARAB EMIRATES

SAUDI ARABIA

OMAN

ABU DHABI

UNITED ARAB EMIRATES

Al Ain

Madinat Zayed

Mazaira

SULTANATE OF OMAN

A B C D

ARABIAN GULF

Ras Musejid

Bu Lifiyat

Ras Al Hadrah

4.8

2.3

3.4 3.1

14.5 4.3

10.1

4.6

5.4 1.7

A b u   A l   A b y a d h   I s l a n d

12

0.8

2

4.3

Tarif

4.6

1.1 E11

5.6

EXIT 282

7

9.3 EXIT 246 1.3 5.7

E11 3 4.5

🄿 **Tarif Police Station**

29

53° 50'

© Explorer Group Ltd. 2013

UAE **Road Atlas** Explorer

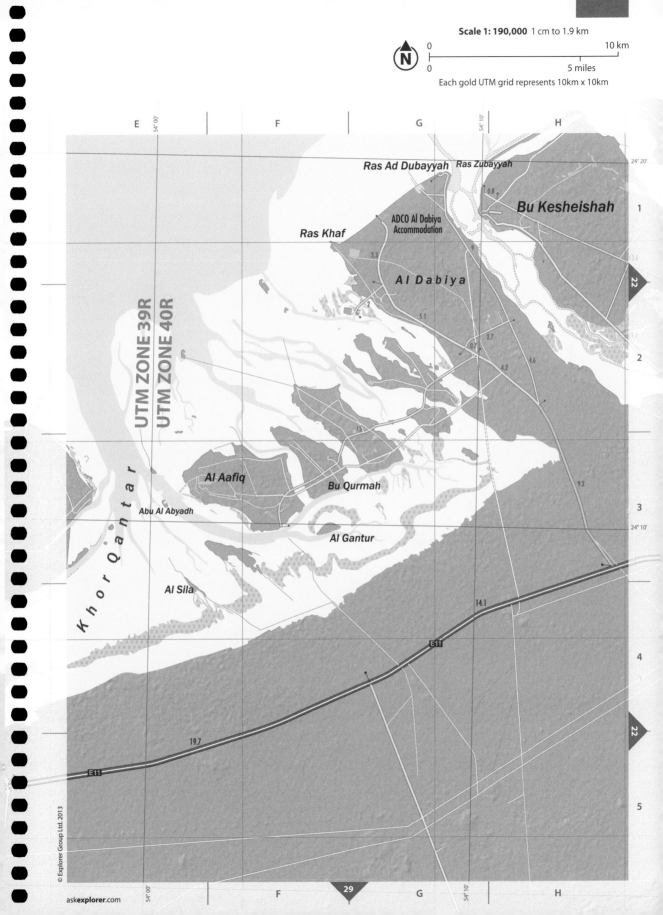

Scale 1: 190,000 1 cm to 1.9 km

Each gold UTM grid represents 10km x 10km

Ras Ad Dubayyah   Ras Zubayyah

Bu Kesheishah

ADCO Al Dabiya
Accommodation

Ras Khaf

Al Dabiya

UTM ZONE 39R
UTM ZONE 40R

Khor Qantar

Al Aafiq

Bu Qurmah

Abu Al Abyadh

Al Gantur

Al Sila

14.1

E11

19.7

E11

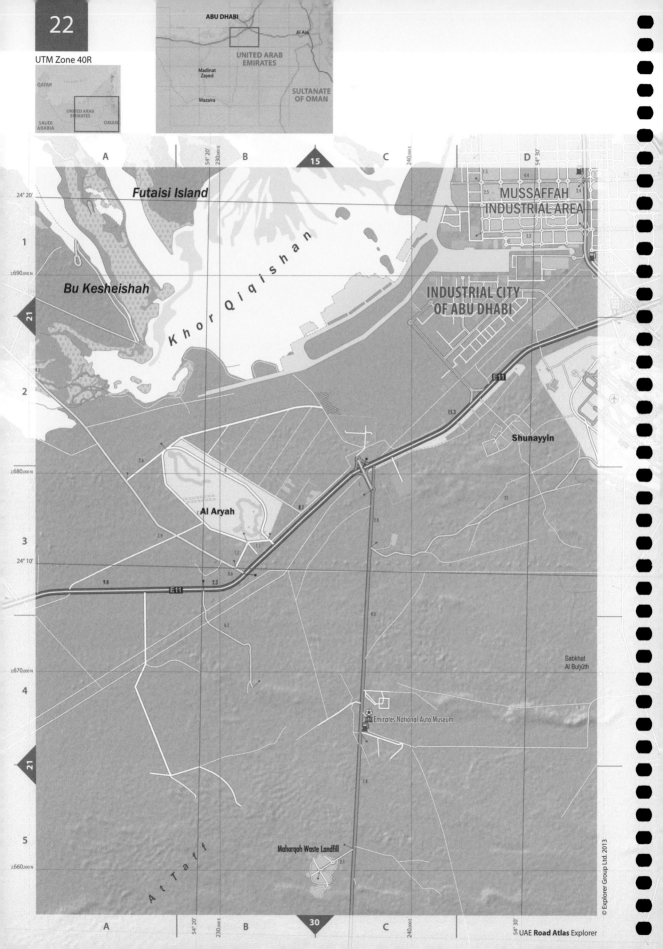

Scale 1: 190,000 1 cm to 1.9 km

0   10 km

0   5 miles

Each gold UTM grid represents 10km x 10km

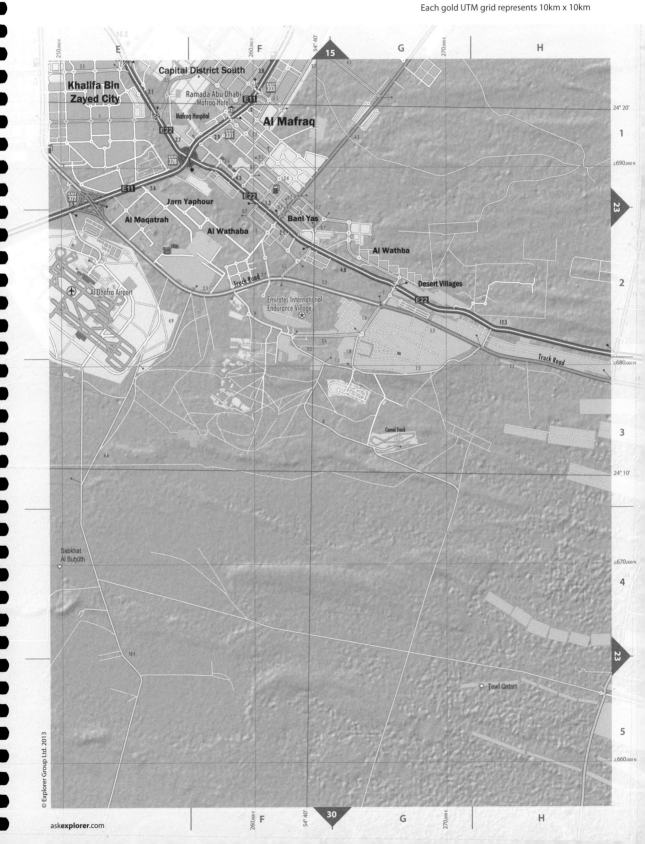

Khalifa Bin Zayed City

Capital District South

Ramada Abu Dhabi Mafraq Hotel

Mafraq Hospital

Al Mafraq

Jarn Yaphour

Al Maqatrah

Al Wathaba

Bani Yas

Al Wathba

Desert Villages

Al Dhafra Airport

Truck Road

Emirates International Endurance Village

Camel Track

Truck Road

Ṣabkhat Al Buḥūth

Ṭawl Qaṭam

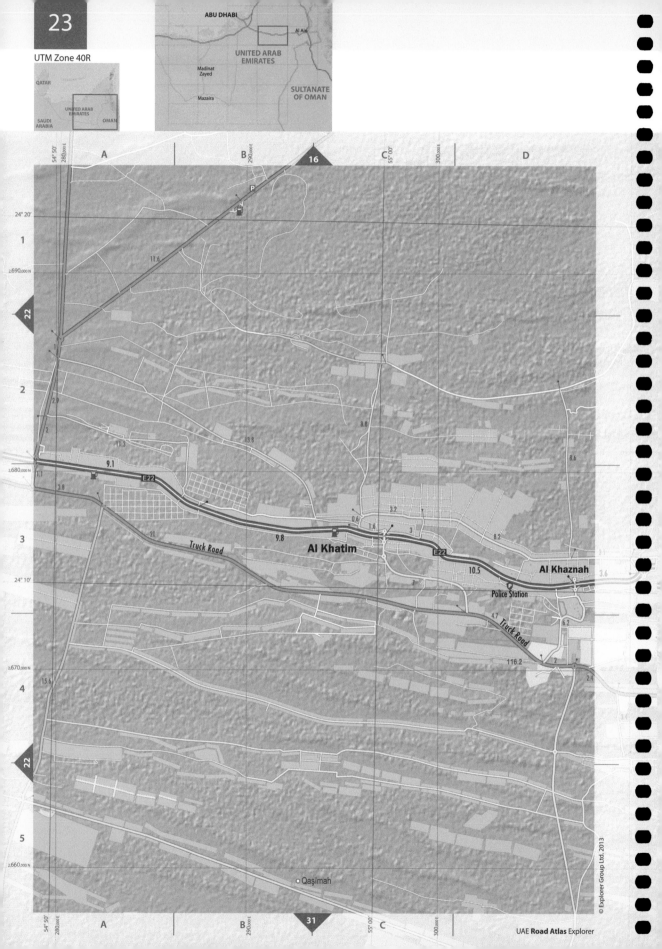

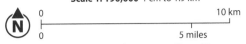

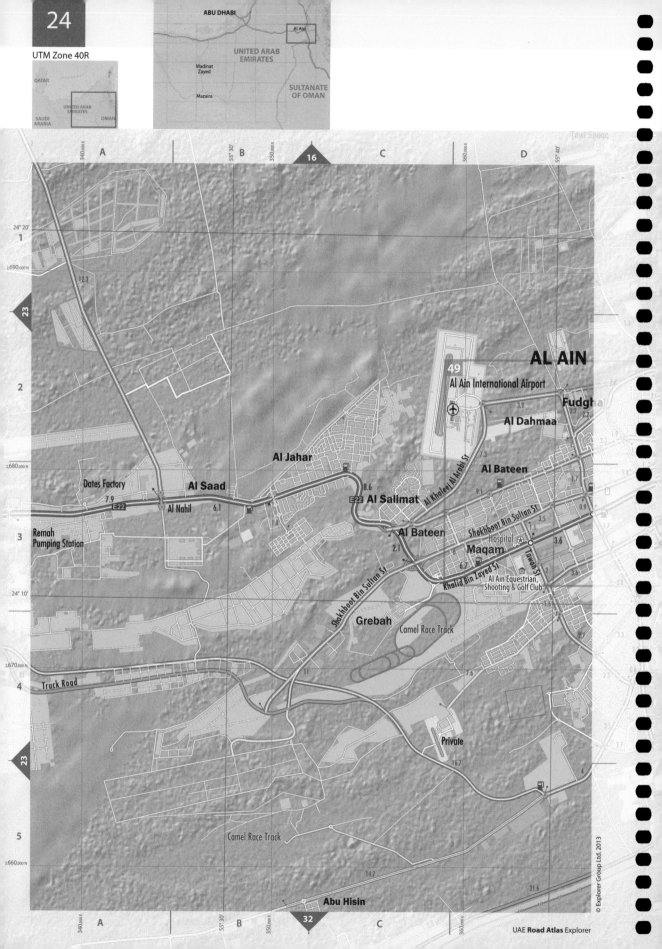

UTM Zone 40R

ABU DHABI

Al Ain

UNITED ARAB
EMIRATES

Madinat
Zayed

SULTANATE
OF OMAN

Mazaira

QATAR

UNITED ARAB
EMIRATES

SAUDI
ARABIA   OMAN

AL AIN

49

Al Ain International Airport

Fudgha

Al Dahmaa

Al Jahar

Al Bateen

Dates Factory   Al Saad

7.9   Al Nahil   6.1

E22

Al Salimat

Al Khaleej Al Arabi St

Remah
Pumping Station

8.6

E22

9.1

Shakhboot Bin Sultan St

Al Bateen

2.1

Hospital

Maqam

3.5

3.6

Shakhboot Bin Sultan St

6.7

Khalid Bin Zayed St

Al Ain Equestrian,
Shooting & Golf Club

Towah St

Grebah

Camel Race Track

11   7.6

Truck Road

Private

16.7

Camel Race Track

14.7

21.6

Abu Hisin

16

32

24° 20'
1

2,690,000 N

12.3

23

2

2,680,000 N

3

24° 10'

2,670,000 N

4

23

5

2,660,000 N

A   B   C   D

340,000 E   55° 30'   350,000 E   360,000 E   55° 40'

UAE **Road Atlas** Explorer

Scale 1: 190,000 1 cm to 1.9 km

0 ——————————————— 10 km
0 ——————————————— 5 miles

Each gold UTM grid represents 10km x 10km

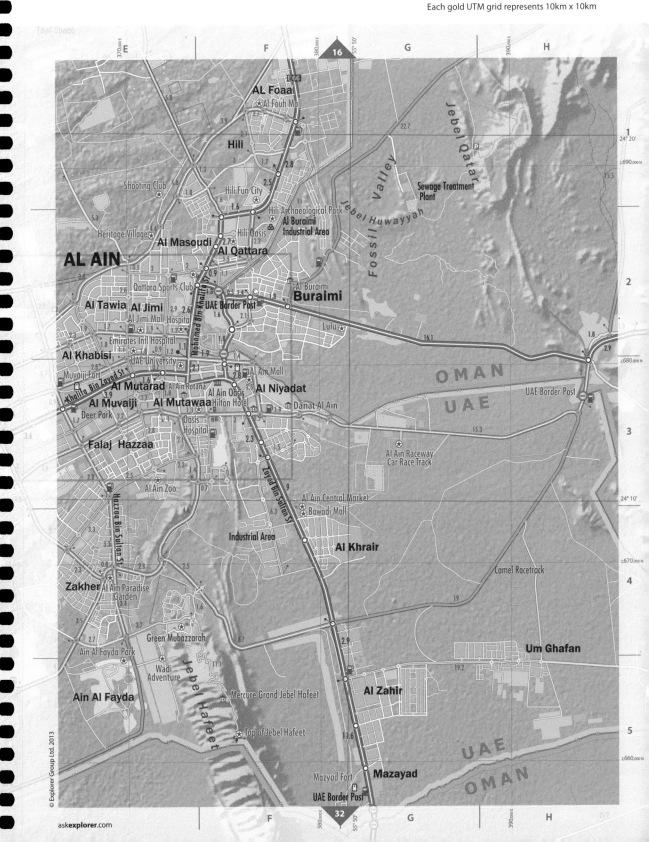

© Explorer Group Ltd. 2013

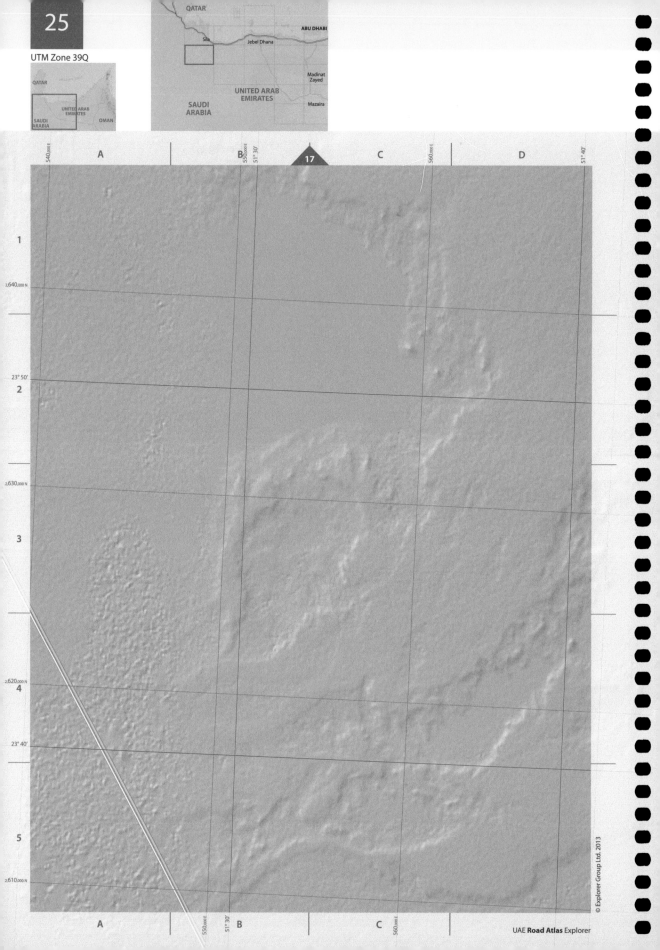

Scale 1: 190,000 1 cm to 1.9 km

0   10 km

0   5 miles

Each gold UTM grid represents 10km x 10km

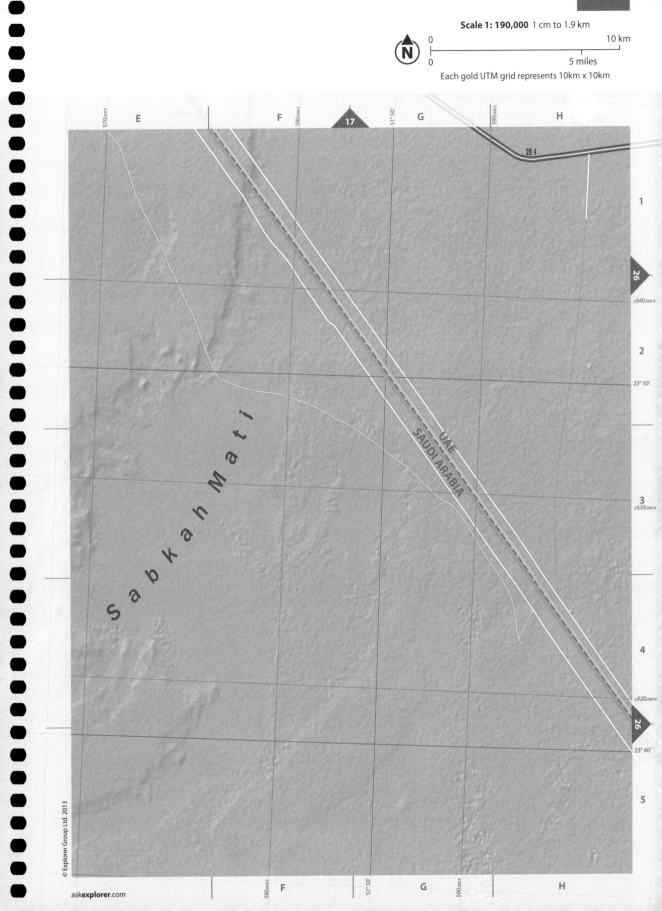

© Explorer Group Ltd. 2013

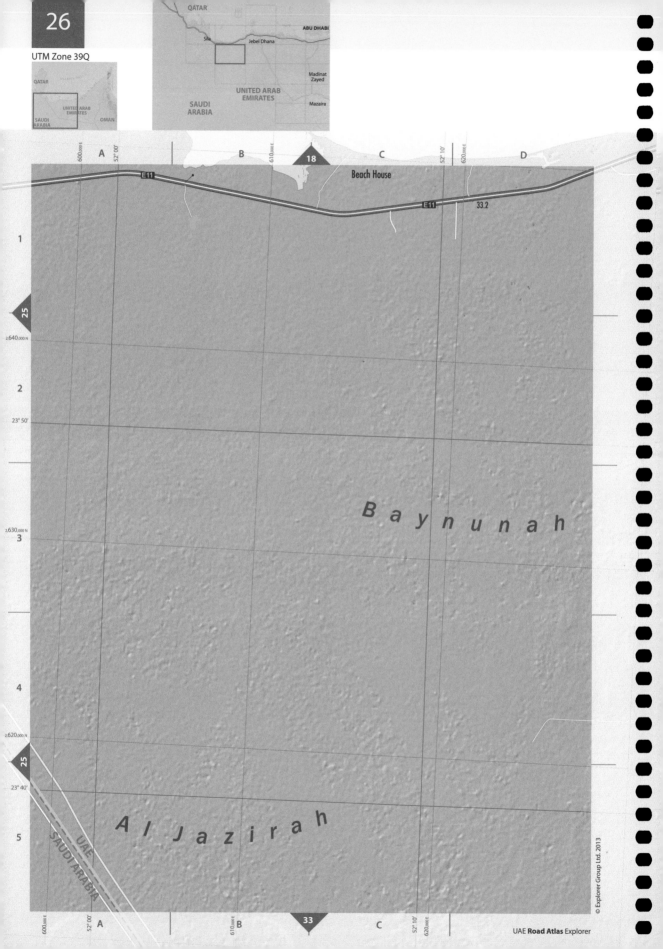

UTM Zone 39Q

QATAR

ABU DHABI

Sila   Jebel Dhana

UNITED ARAB EMIRATES

Madinat Zayed

SAUDI ARABIA

Mazaira

QATAR

UNITED ARAB EMIRATES

SAUDI ARABIA   OMAN

A   B   18   C   D

E11   Beach House

E11   33.2

1

25

2,640,000 N

2

23° 50'

B a y n u n a h

2,630,000 N

3

4

2,620,000 N

25

23° 40'

A l   J a z i r a h

5

UAE

SAUDI ARABIA

600,000 E   52° 00'   A   B   610,000 E   33   C   52° 10'   620,000 E

Scale 1: 190,000 1 cm to 1.9 km

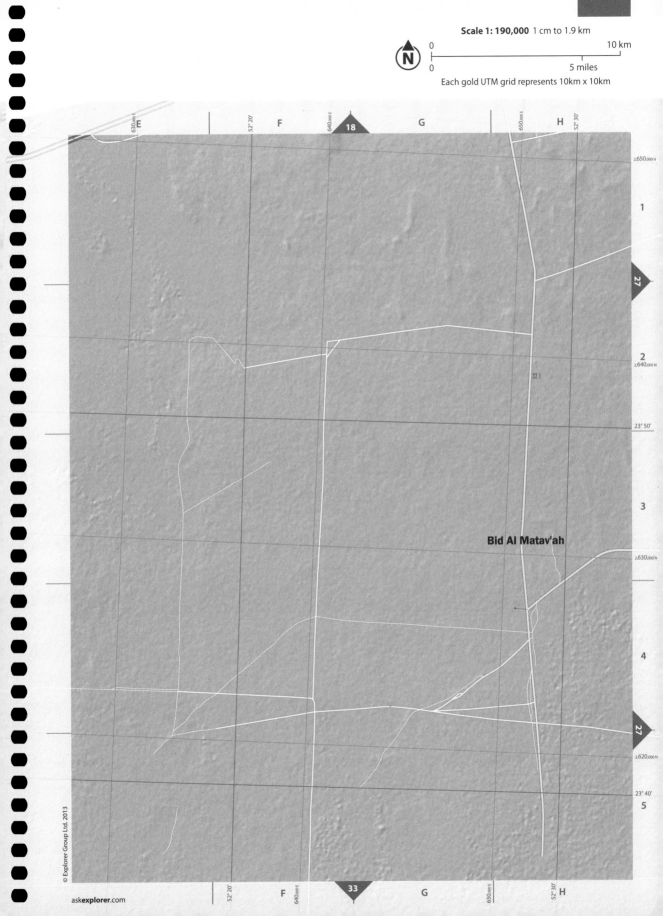

Each gold UTM grid represents 10km x 10km

Bid Al Matav'ah

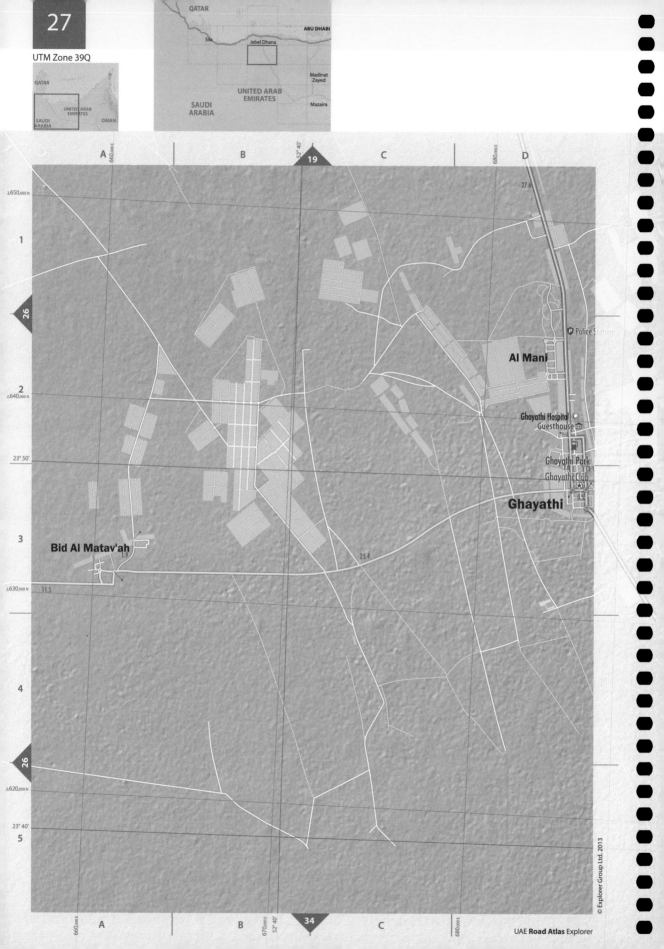

UTM Zone 39Q

QATAR

UNITED ARAB EMIRATES

SAUDI ARABIA

OMAN

QATAR

ABU DHABI

Sila

Jebel Dhana

Madinat Zayed

UNITED ARAB EMIRATES

SAUDI ARABIA

Mazaira

19

A | B | C | D

2,650,000 N

27.6

1

26

Police Station

Al Mani

2

2,640,000 N

Ghayathi Hospital
Guesthouse

23° 50'

Ghayathi Park
Ghayathi Club

Ghayathi

3

Bid Al Matav'ah

25.4

2,630,000 N

11.5

26

4

2,620,000 N

23° 40'

5

© Explorer Group Ltd. 2013

A | B | C

34

52° 40'

Scale 1: 190,000 1 cm to 1.9 km

0   10 km

0   5 miles

Each gold UTM grid represents 10km x 10km

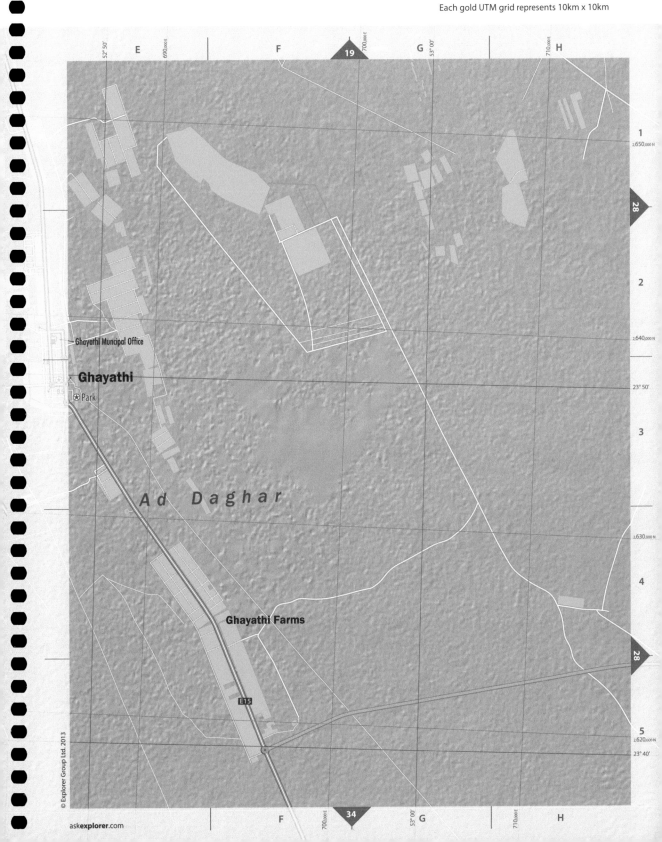

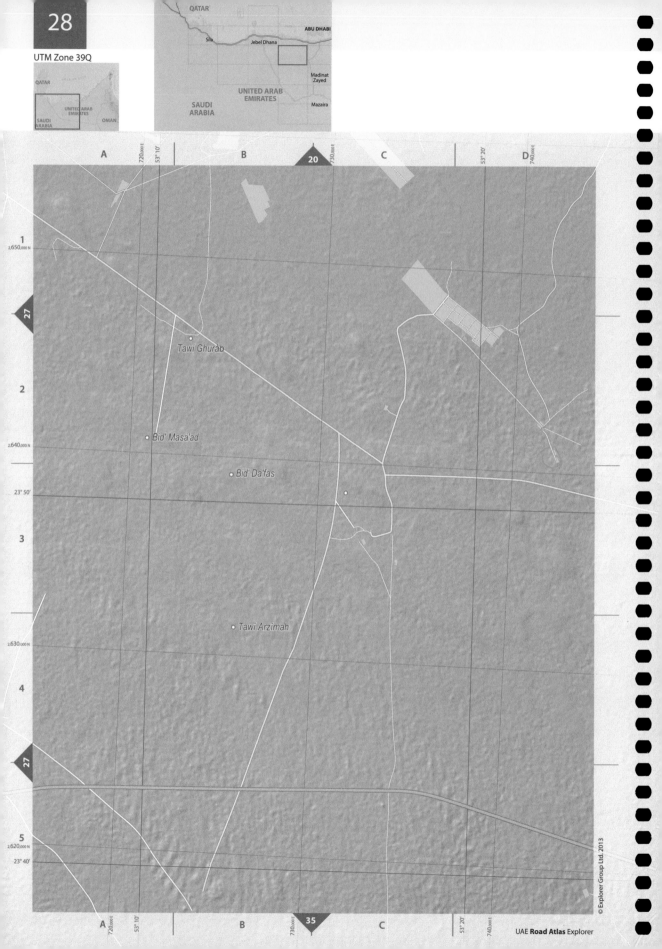

UTM Zone 39Q

QATAR

UNITED ARAB
EMIRATES

SAUDI
ARABIA

OMAN

QATAR

ABU DHABI

Sila

Jebel Dhana

Madinat
Zayed

UNITED ARAB
EMIRATES

SAUDI
ARABIA

Mazaira

Tawi Ghuràb

Bid' Masà'ad

Bid' Da'fas

Tawi Arzimah

© Explorer Group Ltd. 2013

UAE Road Atlas Explorer

Scale 1: 190,000 1 cm to 1.9 km

0   10 km

0   5 miles

Each gold UTM grid represents 10km x 10km

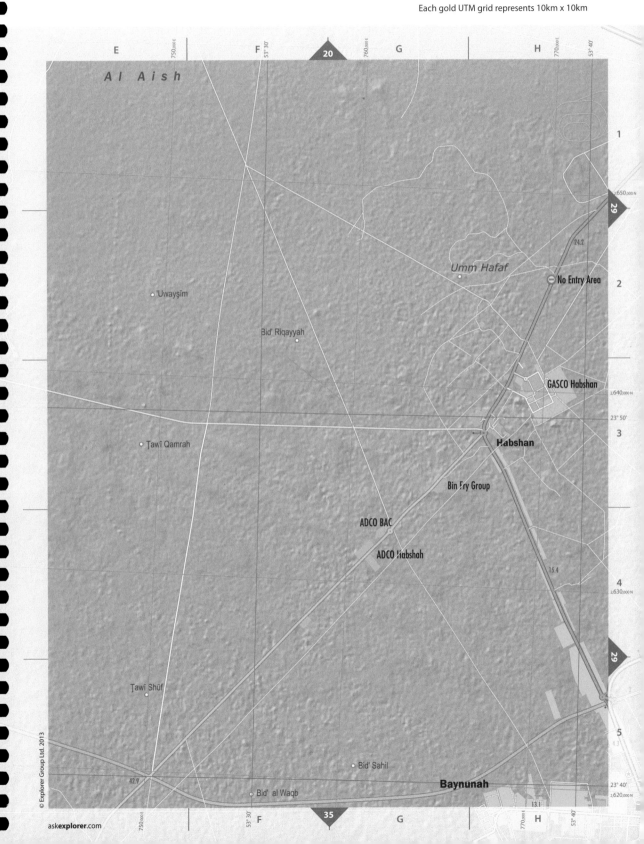

Al Aish

E   750,000 E   F 53° 30'   20   760,000 E   G   H   770,000 E   53° 40'

1

2,650,000 N   29

Umm Hafaf

○ 'Uwayşīm   ⊖ No Entry Area   2

Bid' Riqayyah

GASCO Habshan   2,640,000 N

23° 50'

○ Ţawī Qamrah   Habshan   3

Bin Fry Group

ADCO BAC

ADCO Habshah   4
2,630,000 N

29

○ Ţawī Shūf

5

Bid' Sahil

Baynunah   23° 40'
2,620,000 N

○ Bid' al Waqb   35   G   H

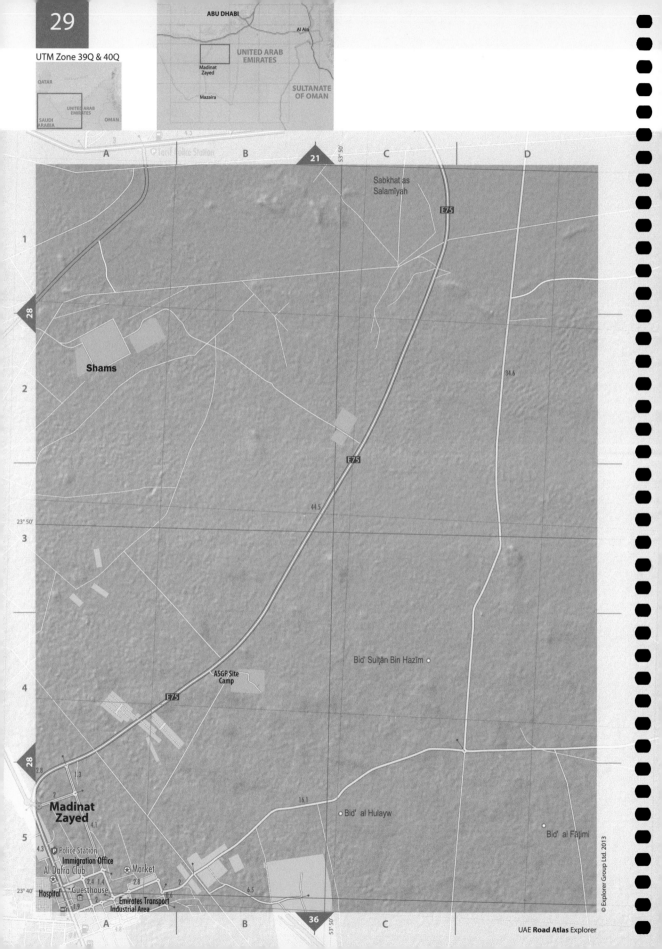

QATAR

UNITED ARAB
EMIRATES

SAUDI
ARABIA   OMAN

ABU DHABI

Al Ain

UNITED ARAB
EMIRATES

Madinat
Zayed

Mazaira

SULTANATE
OF OMAN

A   B   21   C   D

53° 50'

Sabkhat as
Salamīyah

E75

1

28

34.6

Shams

2

E75

23° 50'

44.5

3

Bid' Sulṭān Bin Hazīm

4

ASGP Site
Camp

E75

E75

28

2.8

1.3

2

Madinat
Zayed

4.1

16.1

Bid' al Hulayw

5

Bid' al Fāṭimi

4.3   Police Station
Immigration Office
Al Dafra Club

Market

2.4 1.4

2.8

2

6.5

23° 40'
Hospital   Guesthouse

1.9

Emirates Transport
Industrial Area

2.6

A   B   36   C

53° 50'

Scale 1: 190,000 1 cm to 1.9 km

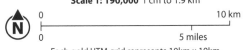

Each gold UTM grid represents 10km x 10km

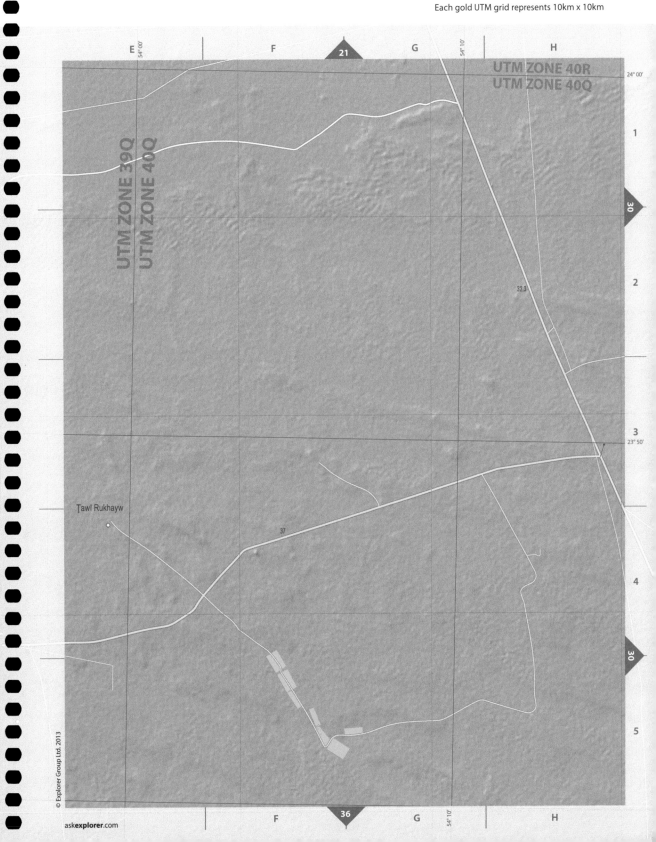

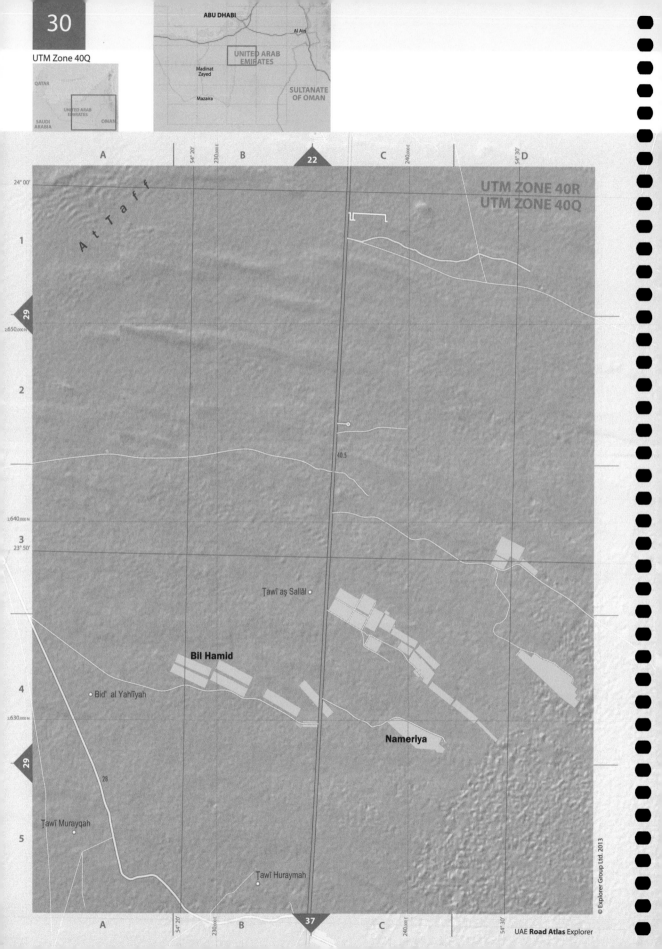

UTM Zone 40Q

ABU DHABI

Al Ain

UNITED ARAB EMIRATES

Madinat Zayed

Mazaira

SULTANATE OF OMAN

QATAR

UNITED ARAB EMIRATES

SAUDI ARABIA

OMAN

A · t · T a f f

UTM ZONE 40R
UTM ZONE 40Q

24° 00'

230,000E
54° 20'

240,000E

54° 30'

22

1

29

2,650,000 N

2

40.5

2,640,000 N

3
23° 50'

Ṭawī aṣ Sallāl

Bil Hamid

4

Bid' al Yahlīyah

2,630,000 N

Nameriya

29

28

Ṭawī Murayqah

5

Ṭawī Huraymah

37

© Explorer Group Ltd. 2013

Scale 1: 190,000 1 cm to 1.9 km

0   10 km

0   5 miles

Each gold UTM grid represents 10km x 10km

© Explorer Group Ltd. 2013

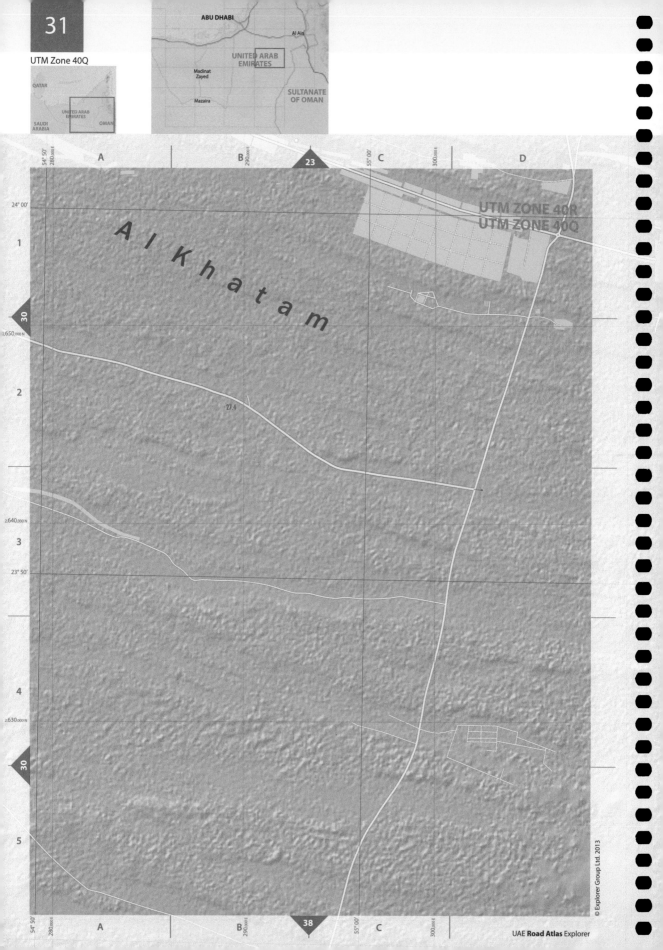

UTM Zone 40Q

ABU DHABI

Al Ain

UNITED ARAB EMIRATES

Madinat
Zayed

SULTANATE
OF OMAN

Mazaira

QATAR

UNITED ARAB
EMIRATES

SAUDI
ARABIA

OMAN

A l   K h a t a m

UTM ZONE 40R
UTM ZONE 40Q

23

24° 00'

55° 00'

300,000 E

280,000 E

290,000 E

54° 50'

1

30

2,650,000 N

2

27.4

2,640,000 N

3

23° 50'

4

2,630,000 N

30

5

38

A   280,000 E   B   290,000 E   C   300,000 E   54° 50'   55° 00'

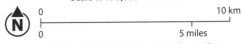

Khuwayr 'Azzān

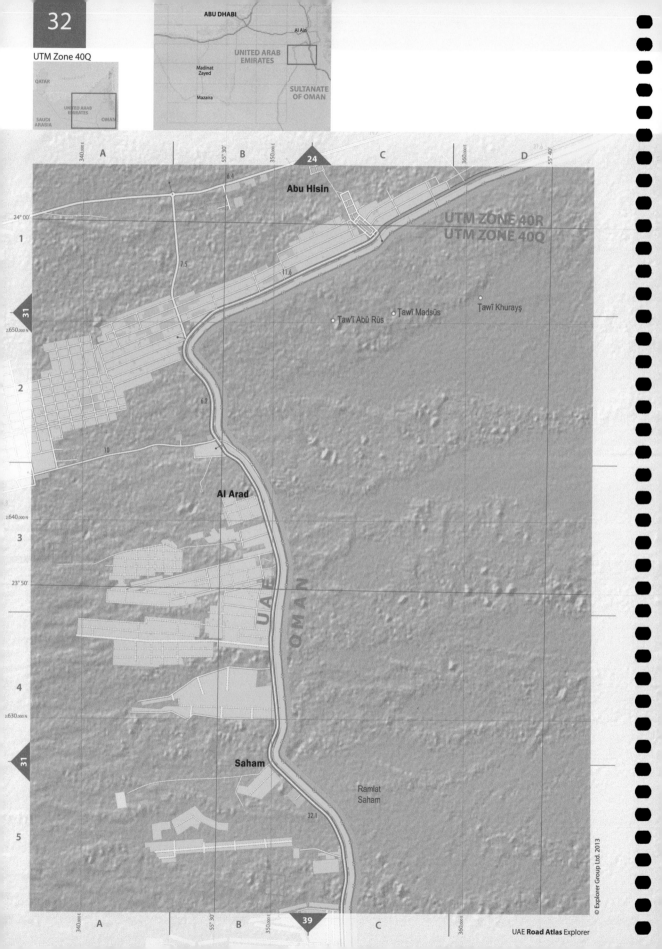

UTM Zone 40Q

ABU DHABI

Al Ain

UNITED ARAB
EMIRATES

QATAR

UNITED ARAB
EMIRATES

OMAN

SAUDI
ARABIA

Madinat
Zayed

Mazaira

SULTANATE
OF OMAN

A   340,000 E   B   55° 30'   350,000 E   C   360,000 E   D   55° 40'

24

Abu Hisin

6.4

24° 00'

1

UTM ZONE 40R
UTM ZONE 40Q

7.5

11.6

31

Ṭawī Khurayş

2,650,000 N

Ṭawī Abū Rūs   Ṭawī Madsūs

2

6.2

10

Al Arad

2,640,000 N

3

23° 50'

UAE

OMAN

4

2,630,000 N

31

Saham

Ramlat
Saham

32.1

5

© Explorer Group Ltd. 2013

A   340,000 E   B   55° 30'   350,000 E   39   C   360,000 E

Scale 1: 190,000 1 cm to 1.9 km

0 _____ 10 km

0 _____ 5 miles

Each gold UTM grid represents 10km x 10km

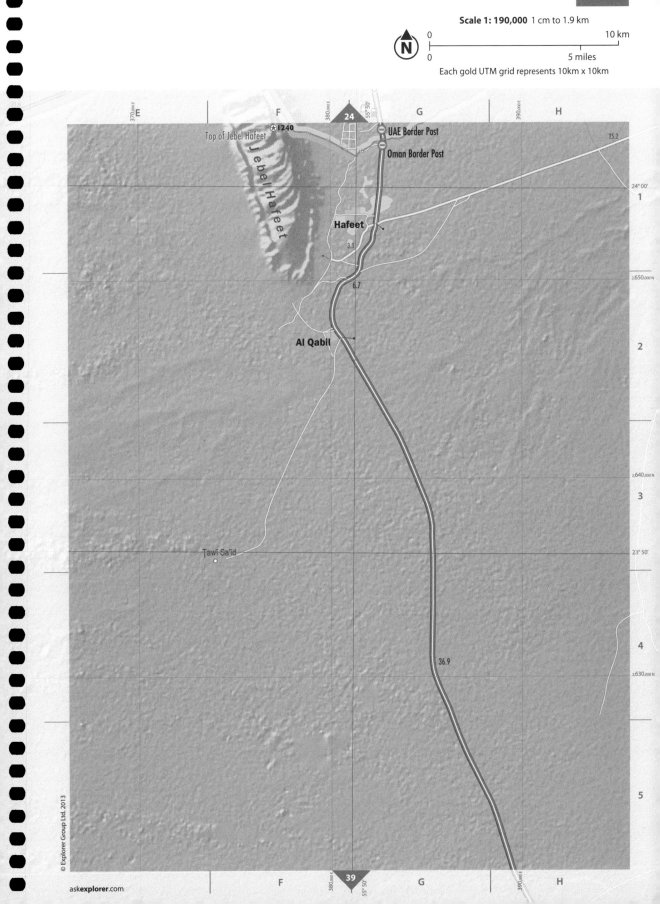

© Explorer Group Ltd. 2013

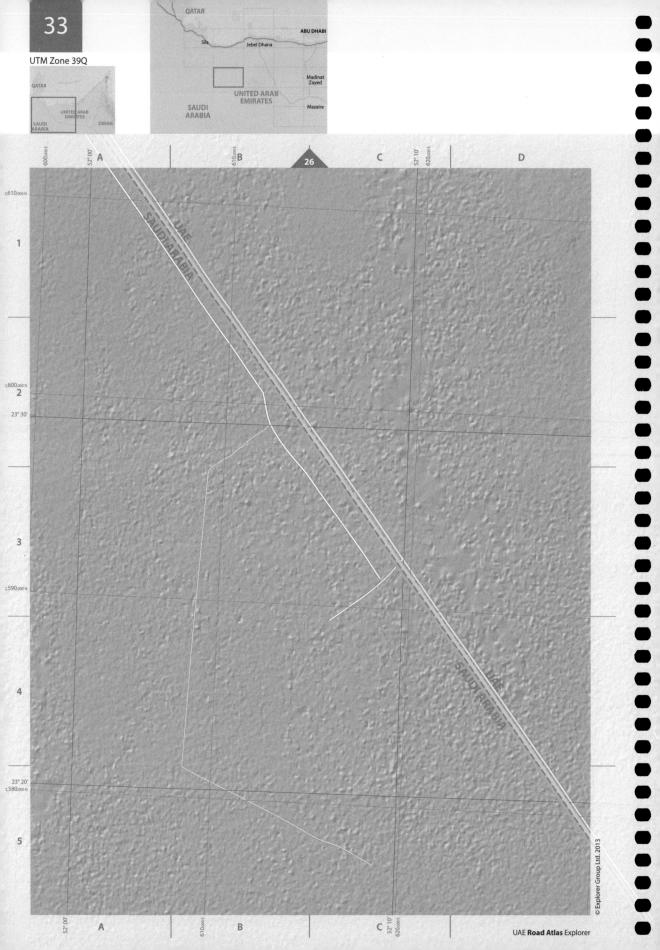

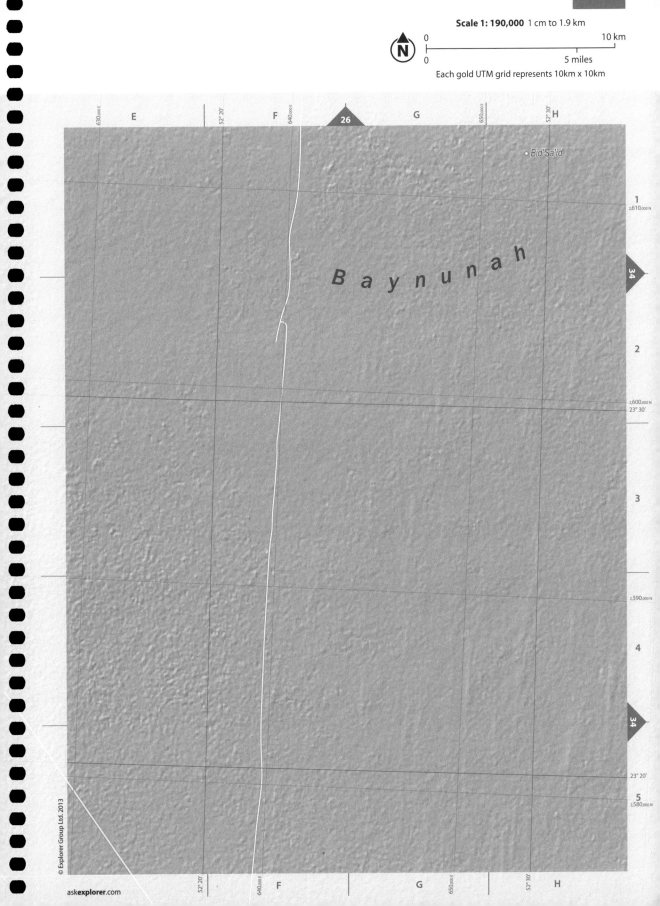

Scale 1: 190,000 1 cm to 1.9 km

N

0　　　　　　　　　　　　　　　　　　　　　10 km

0　　　　　　　　　　　　　　　5 miles

Each gold UTM grid represents 10km x 10km

E　　　　52° 20'　　　F　　　26　　　G　　　　52° 30'　H

630,000 E　　　　　　　640,000 E　　　　　　650,000 E

• Bid'Sa'id

Baynunah

1
2,610,000 N

34

2

2,600,000 N
23° 30'

3

2,590,000 N

4

34

23° 20'

5
2,580,000 N

52° 20'　　F　　640,000 E　　　G　650,000 E　　52° 30'　H

UTM Zone 39Q

QATAR

UNITED ARAB
EMIRATES

SAUDI
ARABIA
OMAN

QATAR

ABU DHABI

Sila   Jebel Dhana

Madinat
Zayed

UNITED ARAB
EMIRATES

SAUDI
ARABIA

Mazaira

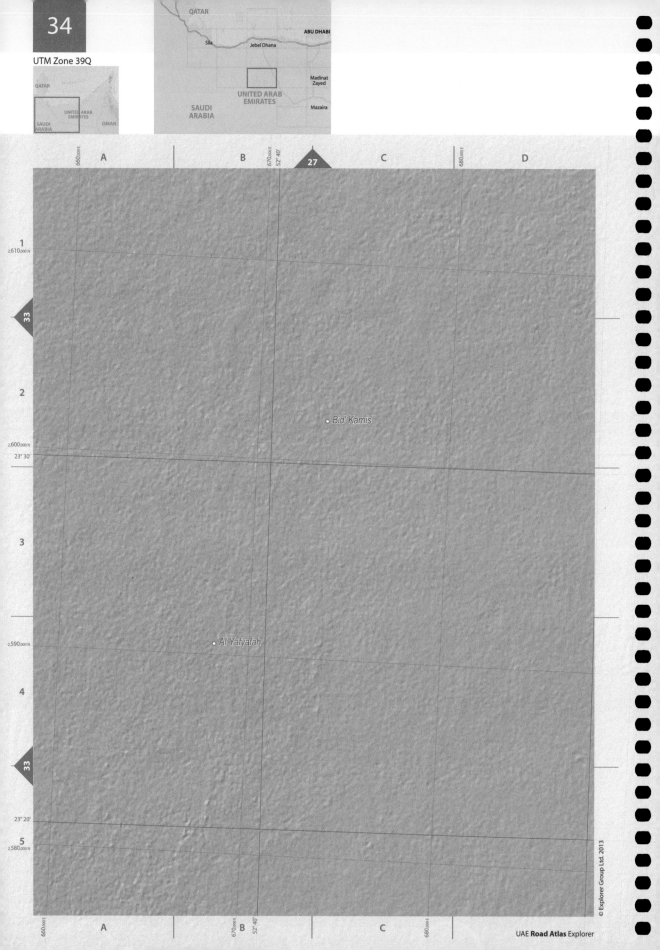

A   B   27   C   D

1

33

2

○ *Bid' Kamis*

3

○ *Al Yafyafah*

4

33

5

A   B   C

Scale 1: 190,000 1 cm to 1.9 km

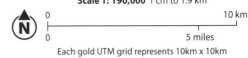

0   10 km

0   5 miles

Each gold UTM grid represents 10km x 10km

© Explorer Group Ltd. 2013

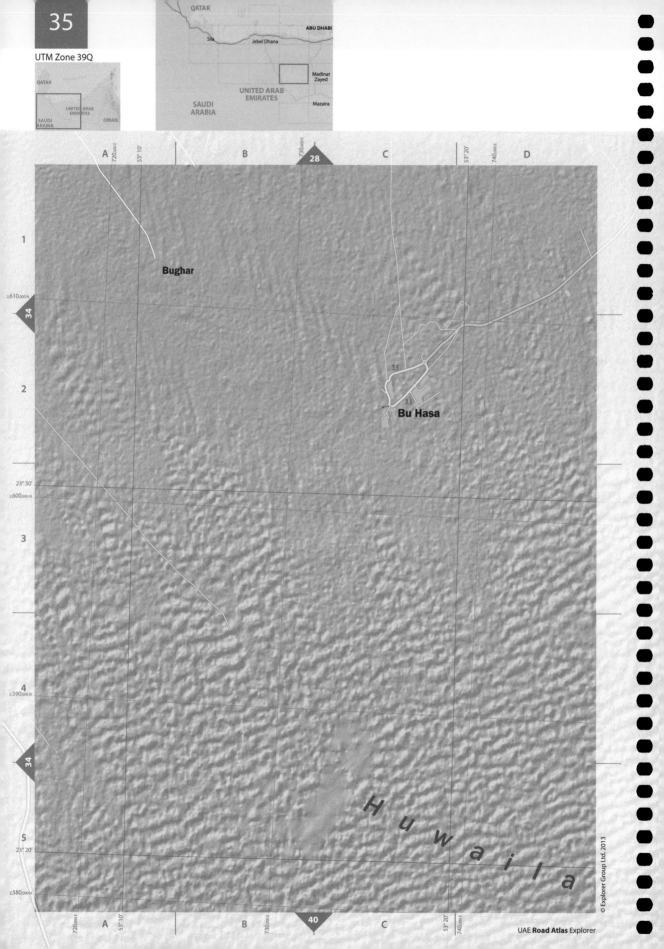

UTM Zone 39Q

QATAR

ABU DHABI

Sila

Jebel Dhana

Madinat
Zayed

UNITED ARAB
EMIRATES

SAUDI
ARABIA

Mazaira

QATAR

UNITED ARAB
EMIRATES

SAUDI
ARABIA

OMAN

A   B   28   C   D

Bughar

Bu Hasa

3.5

3.1

Huwaila

© Explorer Group Ltd. 2013

A   B   40   C

E   53° 30'   F   28   G   H   53° 40'

750,000 E   760,000 E   770,000 E

Bid' al Waqb

Baynunah

1

36

2,610,000 N

2

○ Ţawī Khabb al Hatham

○ Ţawī Khabb al Qirūn

23° 30'

O i l f i e l d   A r e a

3

2,600,000 N

○ Bid' Wāsiţ

4

2,590,000 N

A l   Q a f a

36

5

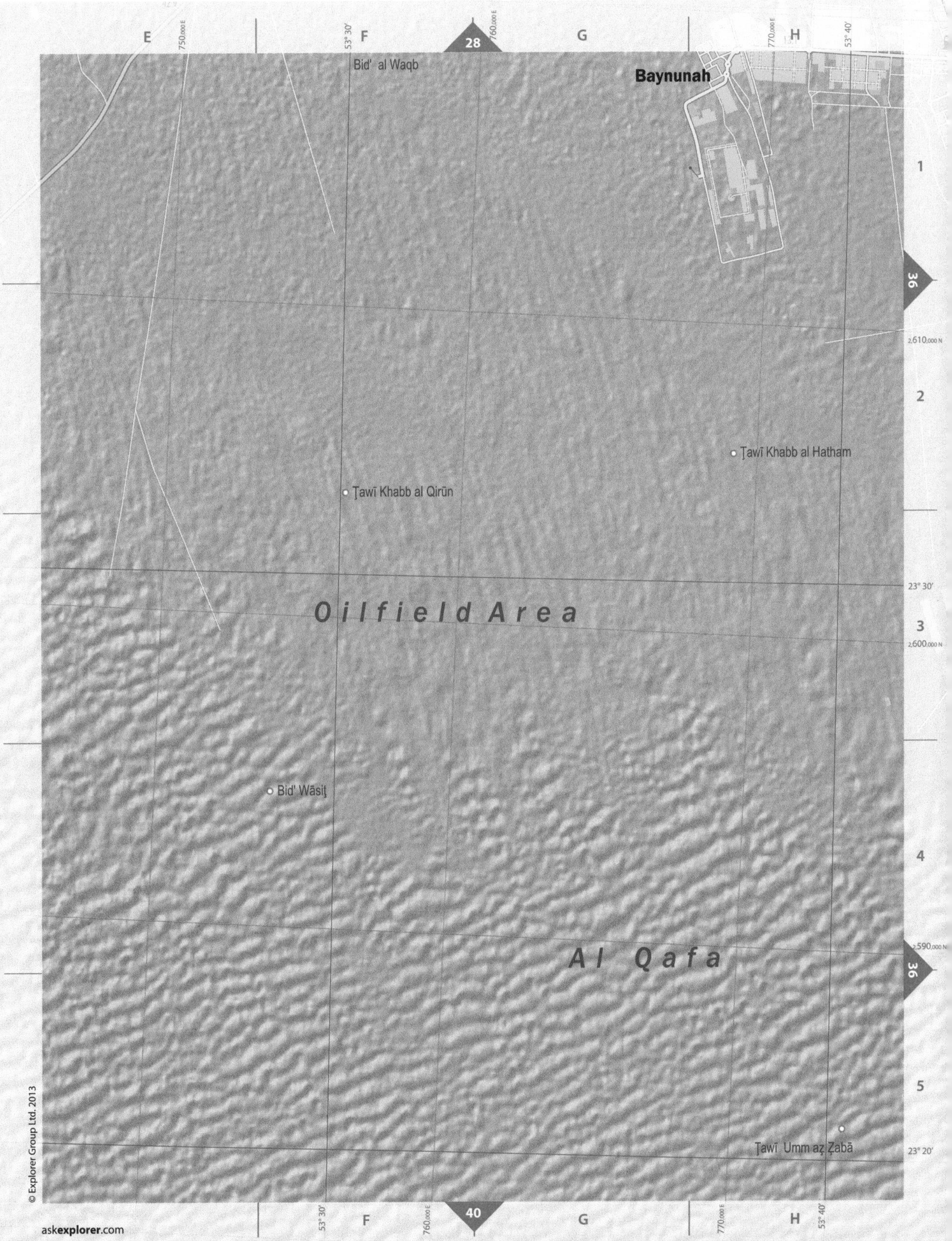

○ Ţawī Umm aẓ Ẕabā

23° 20'

53° 30'   F   760,000 E   40   G   770,000 E   H   53° 40'

UTM Zone 39Q & 40Q

QATAR

UNITED ARAB EMIRATES

SAUDI ARABIA

OMAN

ABU DHABI

Al Ain

UNITED ARAB EMIRATES

Madinat Zayed

Mazaira

SULTANATE OF OMAN

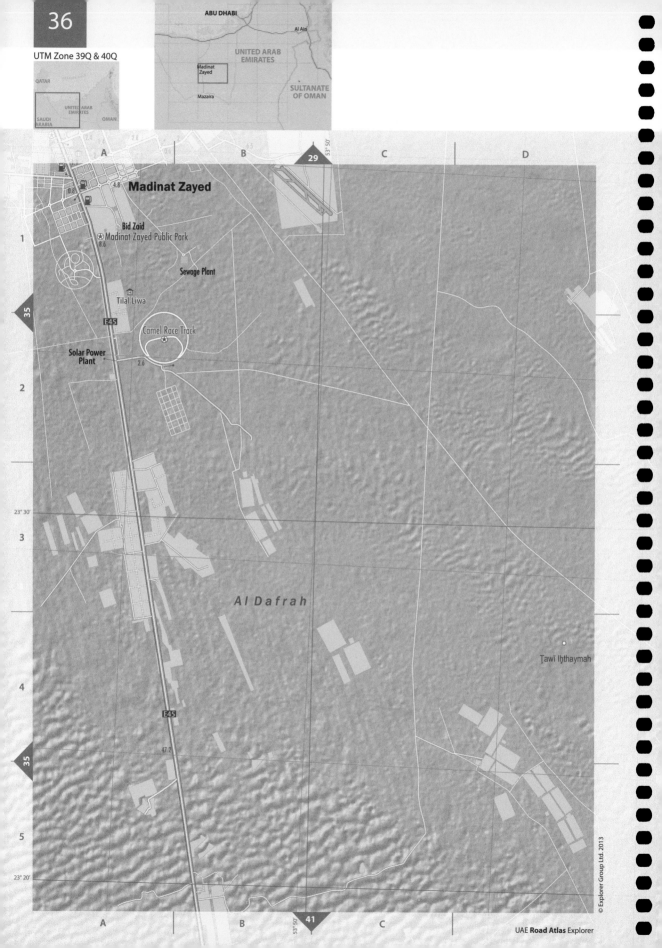

A | B | 29 | C | D

53° 50'

Madinat Zayed

Bid Zaid
⊛ Madinat Zayed Public Park
8.6

Sewage Plant

1

35

Tilal Liwa

E45

Camel Race Track

Solar Power Plant

2.6

2

23° 30'

3

Al Dafrah

Ṭawī Iḥthaymah

4

E45

35

47.2

5

23° 20'

A | B | 41 | C

53° 50'

UAE **Road Atlas** Explorer

© Explorer Group Ltd. 2013

Ṭawī Bū Ḥiyāy

UTM ZONE 39Q
UTM ZONE 40Q

UTM Zone 40Q

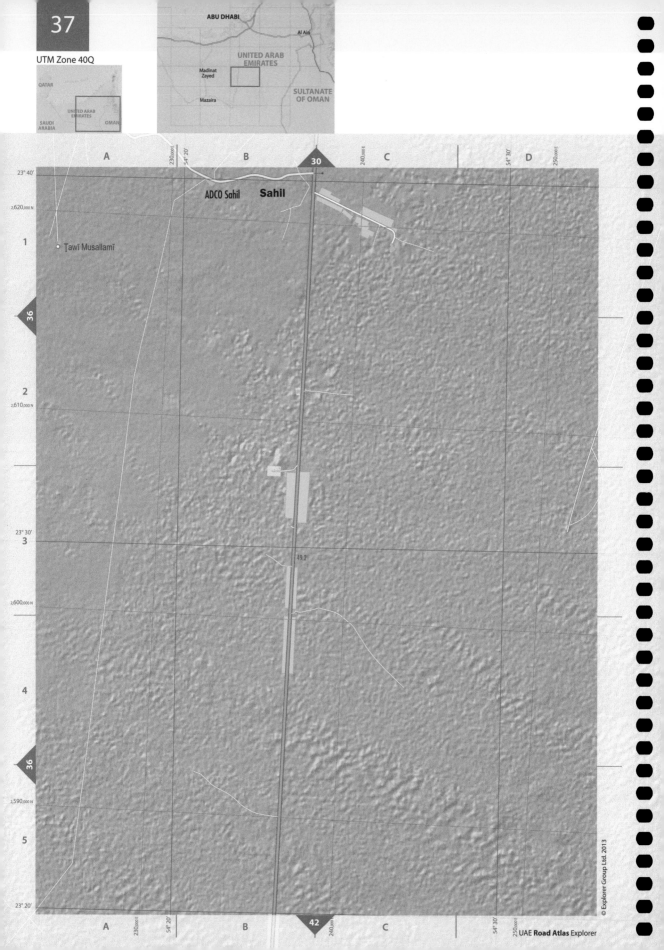

ABU DHABI

Al Ain

UNITED ARAB
EMIRATES

Madinat
Zayed

Mazaira

SULTANATE
OF OMAN

QATAR

UNITED ARAB
EMIRATES

OMAN

SAUDI
ARABIA

ADCO Sahil   **Sahil**

Ṭawī Musallamī

49.2

© Explorer Group Ltd. 2013

Scale 1:190,000 1 cm to 1.9 km

0   10 km

0   5 miles

Each gold UTM grid represents 10km x 10km

Al Hamra

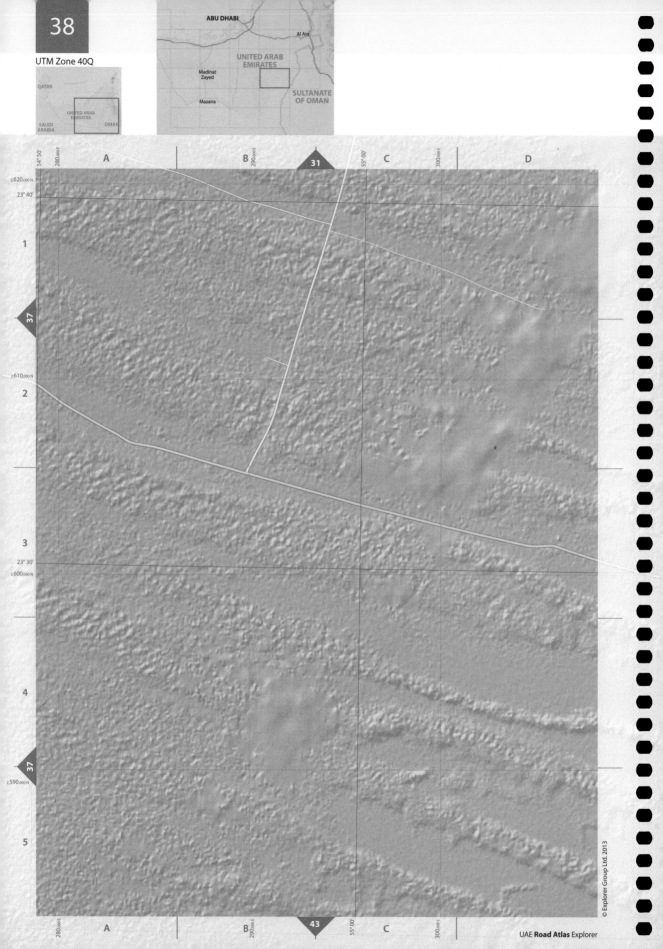

UTM Zone 40Q

ABU DHABI

Al Ain

UNITED ARAB
EMIRATES

Madinat
Zayed

Mazaira

SULTANATE
OF OMAN

QATAR

UNITED ARAB
EMIRATES

SAUDI
ARABIA

OMAN

© Explorer Group Ltd. 2013

Scale 1: 190,000 1 cm to 1.9 km

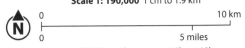

Each gold UTM grid represents 10km x 10km

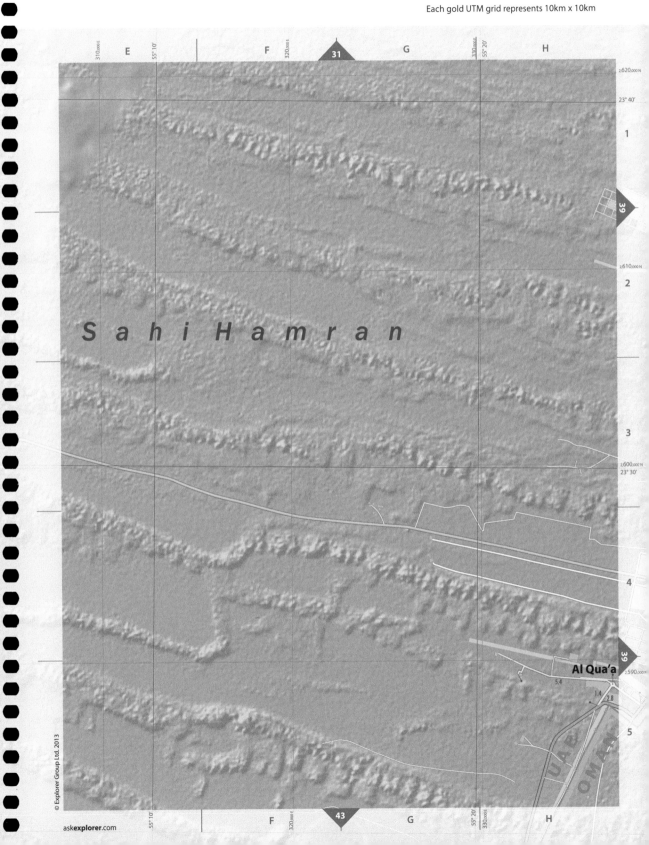

S a h i   H a m r a n

Al Qua'a

ABU DHABI

Al Ain

UNITED ARAB
EMIRATES

Madinat
Zayed

Mazaira

SULTANATE
OF OMAN

QATAR

UNITED ARAB
EMIRATES

SAUDI
ARABIA

OMAN

Al Wijah

Ţawī al Awqān

Camel Racetrack

25

Camel Racetrack

Al Qua'a

6.5

Park

38

Muncipal Office

1.8

© Explorer Group Ltd. 2013

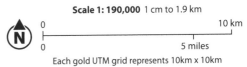

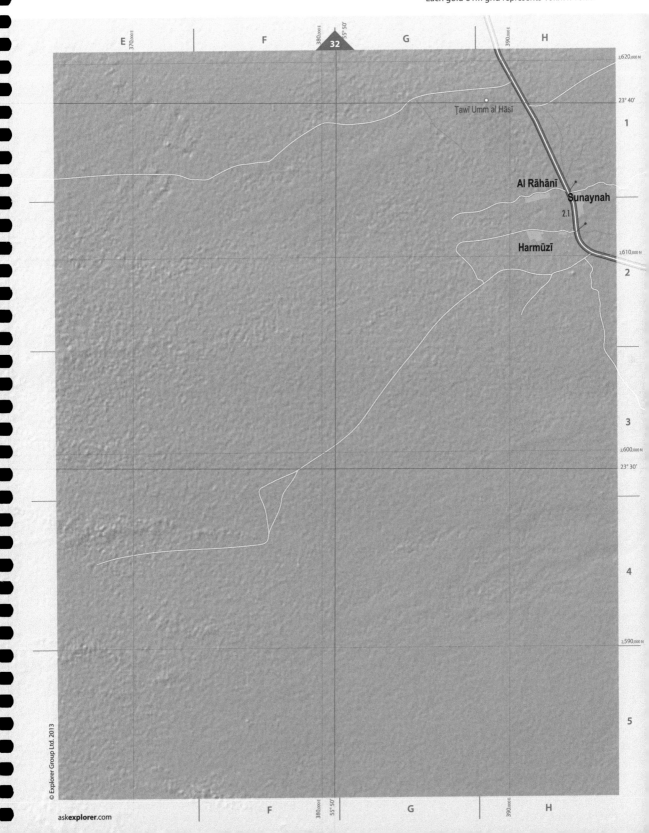

© Explorer Group Ltd. 2013

UTM Zone 39Q

QATAR

SAUDI
ARABIA

UNITED ARAB
EMIRATES

OMAN

QATAR

ABU DHABI

Sila   Jebel Dhana

Madinat
Zayed

SAUDI
ARABIA

UNITED ARAB
EMIRATES

Mazaira

720,000 E   53° 10'   A   B   730,000 E   35   C   53° 20'   740,000 E   D

1

2,570,000 N

2

23° 10'

3
2,560,000 N

E15

4

2,550,000 N

Tawi Bu Ghar

5
23° 00'

720,000 E   53° 10'   A   B   730,000 E   44   C   53° 20'   740,000 E

Arada

© Explorer Group Ltd. 2013

UAE **Road Atlas** Explorer

Scale 1: 190,000 1 cm to 1.9 km

Each gold UTM grid represents 10km x 10km

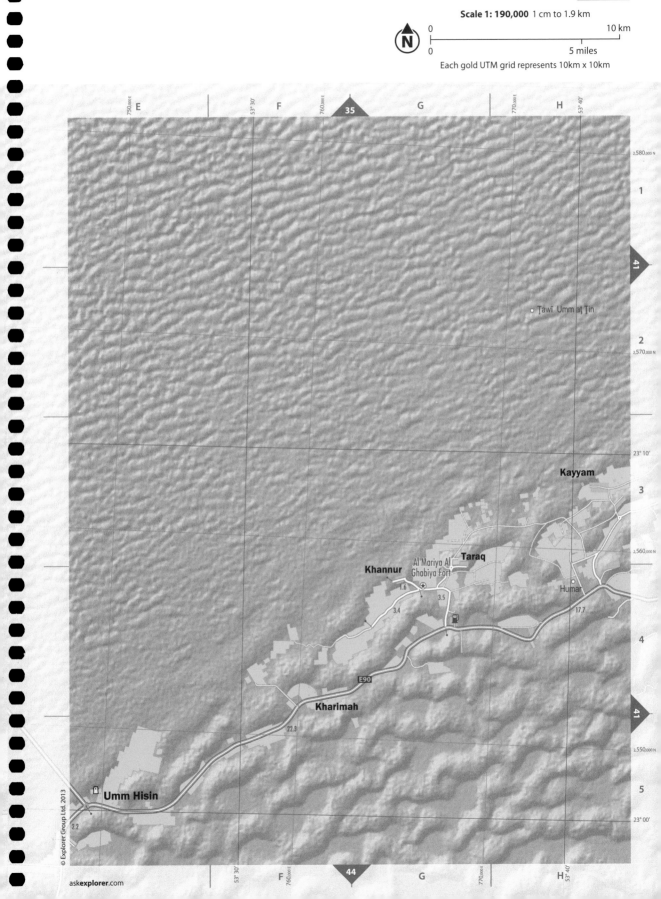

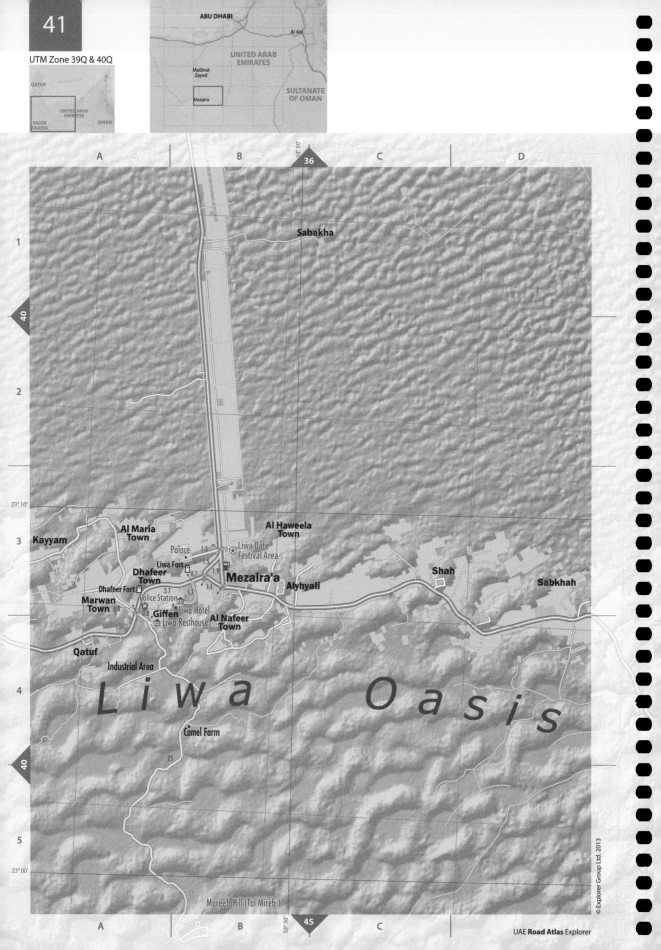

ABU DHABI
Al Ain
UNITED ARAB
EMIRATES
Madinat
Zayed
Mazaira
SULTANATE
OF OMAN

QATAR
UNITED ARAB
EMIRATES
SAUDI ARABIA
OMAN

A | B | 53° 50' 36 | C | D

1

40

2

23° 10'

3

Kayyam

Al Maria
Town

Sabakha

Al Haweela
Town

Palace 1.5
Liwa Date
Festival Area
Liwa Fort 1.5
1.3
Dhafeer
Town 0.7 1.9
Dhafeer Fort Mezaira'a
Police Station Alyhyali
3.7
Marwan
Town 1.8 1.1
0.8 Giffen Liwa Hotel
Liwa Resthouse
Al Nafeer
Town

Shah

Sabkhah

Qatuf

Industrial Area

4

L i w a   O a s i s

Camel Farm

40

25

5

23° 00'

Moreeb Hill (Tal Mireb)

A | B | 53° 50' 45 | C

© Explorer Group Ltd. 2013

Scale 1: 190,000 1 cm to 1.9 km

0   10 km

0   5 miles

Each gold UTM grid represents 10km x 10km

E   F   36   G   H

GASCO Asab

8.0

ADCO Asab

Bid' Hulays

Asab

1

O i l f i e l d A r e a

42

UTM ZONE 39Q
UTM ZONE 40Q

2

R a m a l a t A l H a m r a

Bid' Khalaf

23° 10'

3

Bid' Bū 'Arish

Al Nashash

4

Jarrah

62.3

42

Wedhail

Bid' Mihbil

5

Al Yarya

Al Khis

23° 00'

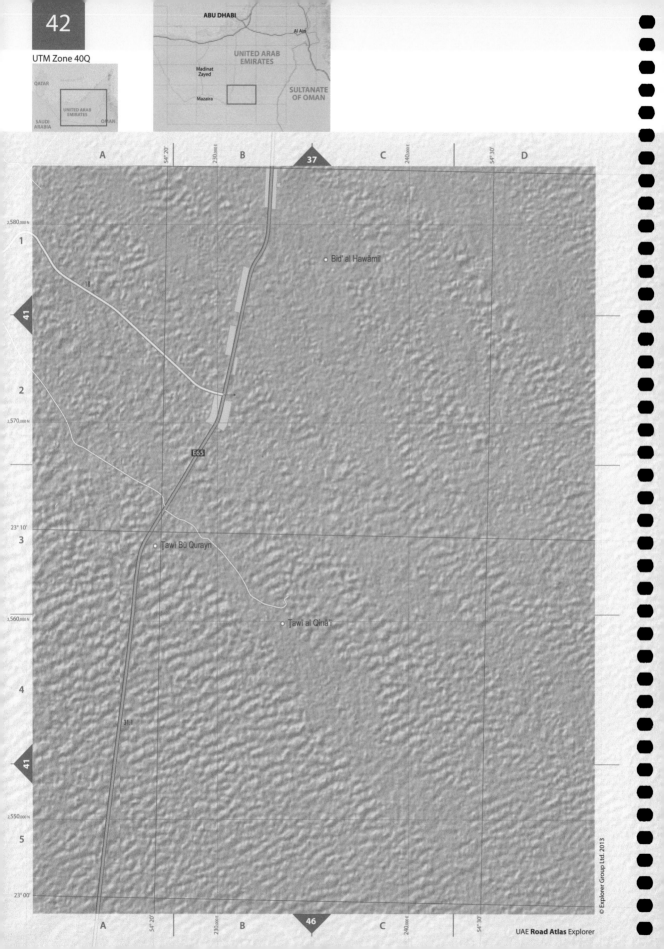

QATAR

UNITED ARAB EMIRATES

SAUDI ARABIA

OMAN

ABU DHABI

Al Ain

UNITED ARAB EMIRATES

Madinat Zayed

Mazaira

SULTANATE OF OMAN

A   54° 20'   230,000 E   B   37   C   240,000 E   54° 30'   D

2,580,000 N

1

○ Bid' al Hawāmil

18

41

2

2,570,000 N

E65

23° 10'

3

○ Ṭawī Bū Qurayn

2,560,000 N

○ Ṭawī al Qinā'ī

4

31.1

41

2,550,000 N

5

23° 00'

A   54° 20'   230,000 E   B   46   C   240,000 E   54° 30'

© Explorer Group Ltd. 2013

Scale 1: 190,000 1 cm to 1.9 km

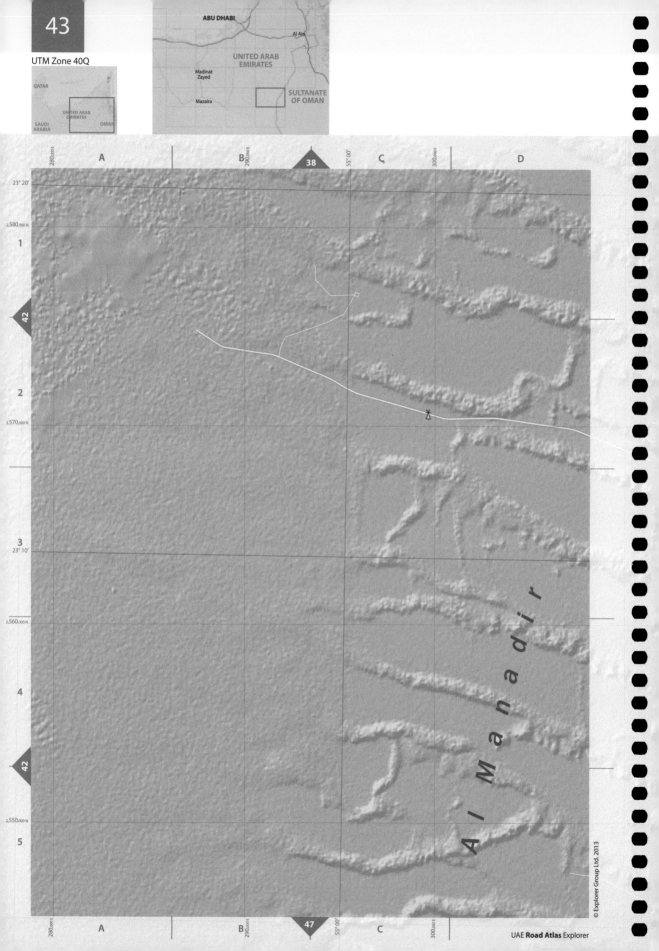

UTM Zone 40Q

QATAR

SAUDI ARABIA

UNITED ARAB EMIRATES

OMAN

ABU DHABI

Al Ain

UNITED ARAB EMIRATES

Madinat Zayed

Mazaira

SULTANATE OF OMAN

A   B   38   C   D

280,000 E   290,000 E   55° 00'   300,000 E

23° 20'

2,580,000 N

1

42

2

2,570,000 N

3
23° 10'

2,560,000 N

4

42

2,550,000 N

5

A l   M a n a d i r

© Explorer Group Ltd. 2013

280,000 E   A   290,000 E   B   47   55° 00'   C   300,000 E

Scale 1: 190,000 1 cm to 1.9 km

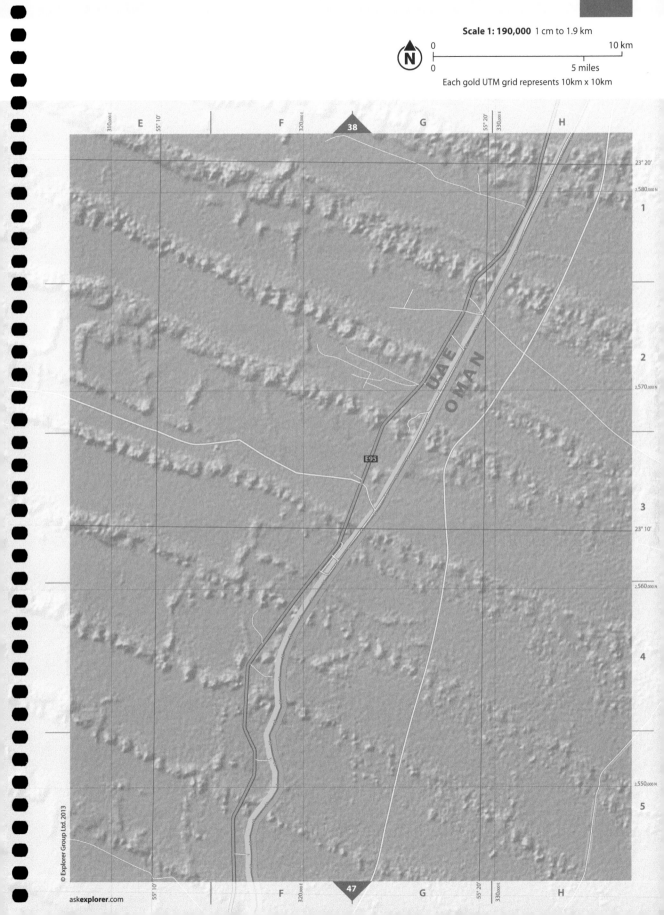

UTM Zone 39Q

QATAR

ABU DHABI

Sila

Jebel Dhana

Madinat
Zayed

UNITED ARAB
EMIRATES

SAUDI
ARABIA

Mazaira

QATAR

UNITED ARAB
EMIRATES

SAUDI
ARABIA

OMAN

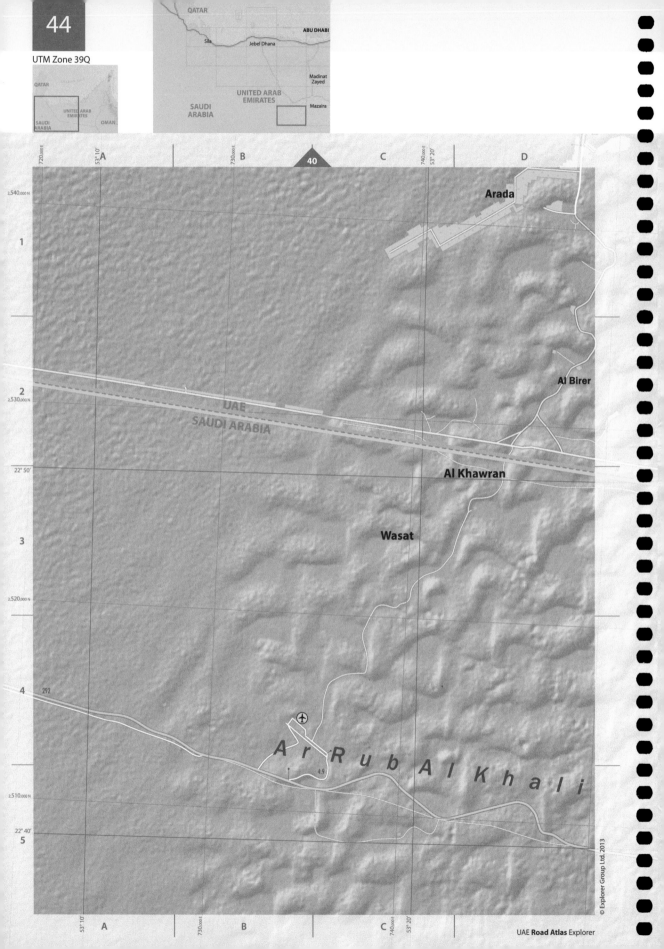

Arada

Al Birer

Al Khawran

Wasat

A r   R u b   A l   K h a l i

292

4.9

40

720,000 E

53° 10'

A

730,000 E

B

740,000 E

53° 20'

C

D

2,540,000 N

1

2

2,530,000 N

UAE

SAUDI ARABIA

22° 50'

3

2,520,000 N

4

2,510,000 N

22° 40'

5

53° 10'

A

730,000 E

B

740,000 E

53° 20'

C

© Explorer Group Ltd. 2013

Scale 1: 190,000 1 cm to 1.9 km

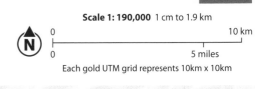

Each gold UTM grid represents 10km x 10km

© Explorer Group Ltd. 2013

UTM Zone 39Q & 40Q

ABU DHABI

Al Ain

UNITED ARAB
EMIRATES

Madinat
Zayed

Mazaira

SULTANATE
OF OMAN

A   B   53° 50' **41**   C   D

Moreeb Hill (Tal Mireb)

Oilfield Area

1

44

S h a h

2

22° 50'

3

UAE

SAUDI ARABIA

4

44

5

22° 40'

A   B   53° 50'   C

© Explorer Group Ltd. 2013

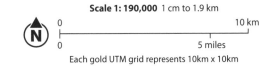

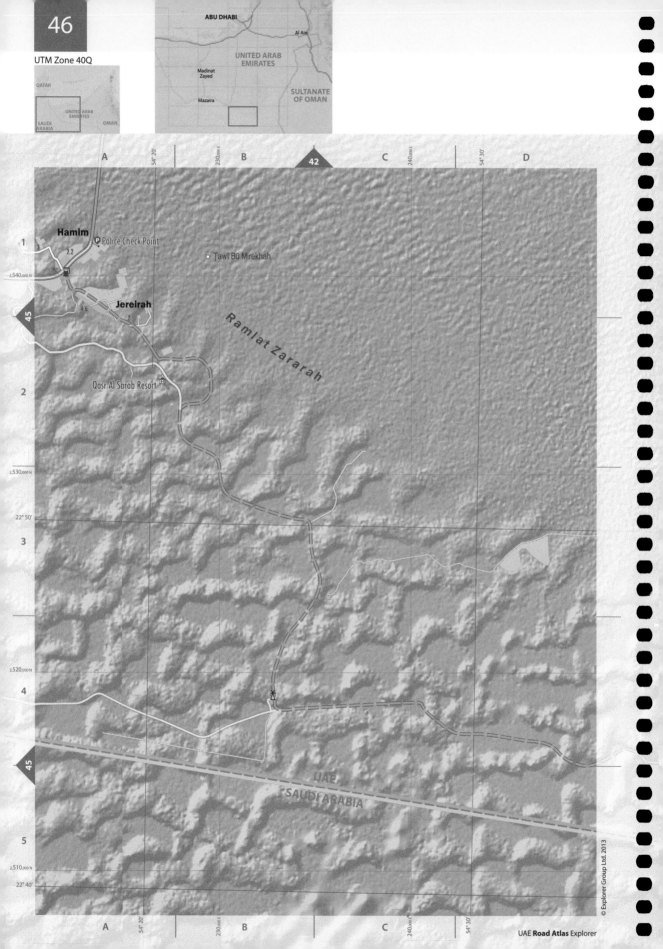

UTM Zone 40Q

QATAR

UNITED ARAB EMIRATES

SAUDI ARABIA

OMAN

ABU DHABI

Al Ain

UNITED ARAB EMIRATES

Madinat Zayed

Mazaira

SULTANATE OF OMAN

42

A   54° 20'   230,000 E   B   C   240,000 E   54° 30'   D

Hamīm

Police Check Point

Ṭawī Bū Mirekhah

2.540,000 N

45

4.6

Jereirah

Qasr Al Sarab Resort

Ramlat Zararah

1

2

2.530,000 N

22° 50'

3

2.520,000 N

4

45

UAE

SAUDI ARABIA

5

2.510,000 N

22° 40'

A   54° 20'   230,000 E   B   C   240,000 E   54° 30'

© Explorer Group Ltd. 2013

Scale 1: 190,000 1 cm to 1.9 km

N

0   10 km

0   5 miles

Each gold UTM grid represents 10km x 10km

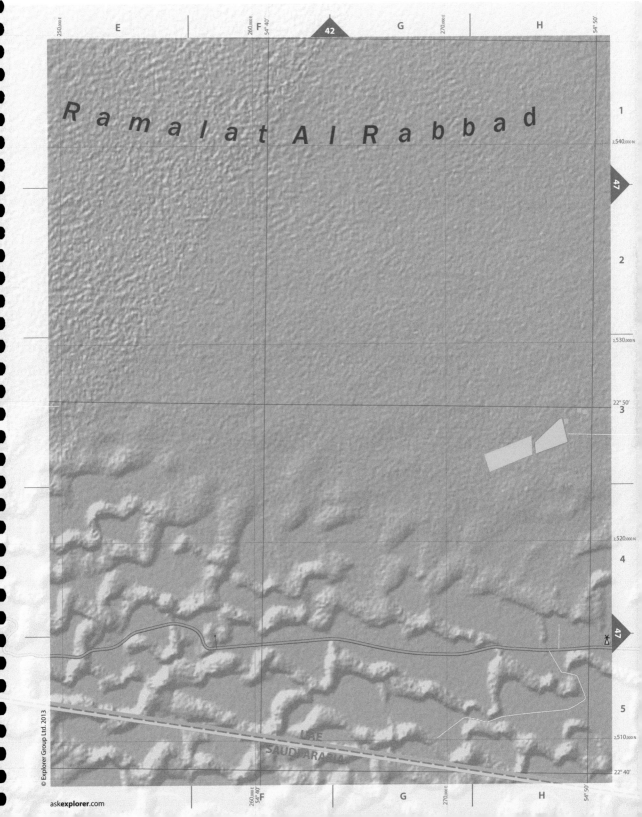

R a m a l a t   A l   R a b b a d

UAE
SAUDI ARABIA

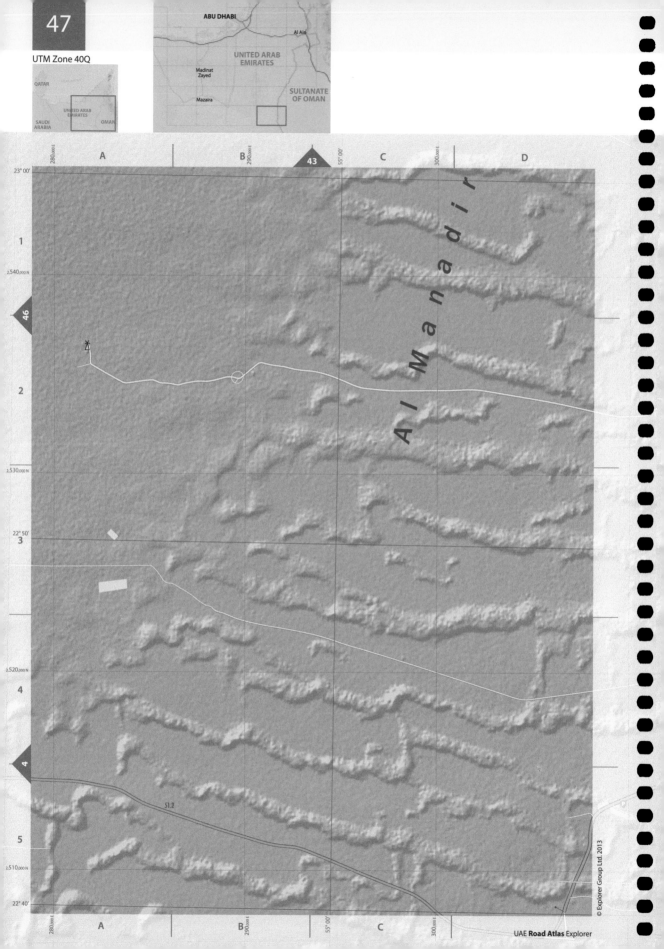

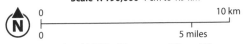

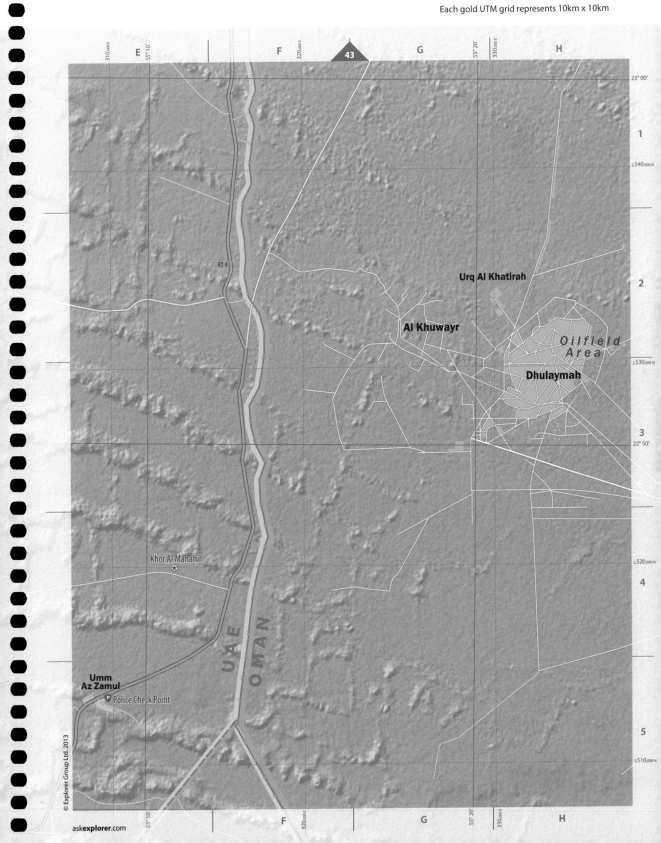

Urq Al Khatirah

Al Khuwayr

Oilfield Area

Dhulaymah

Khor Al Manahil

U.A.E

OMAN

Umm Az Zamul

Police Check Point

© Explorer Group Ltd. 2013

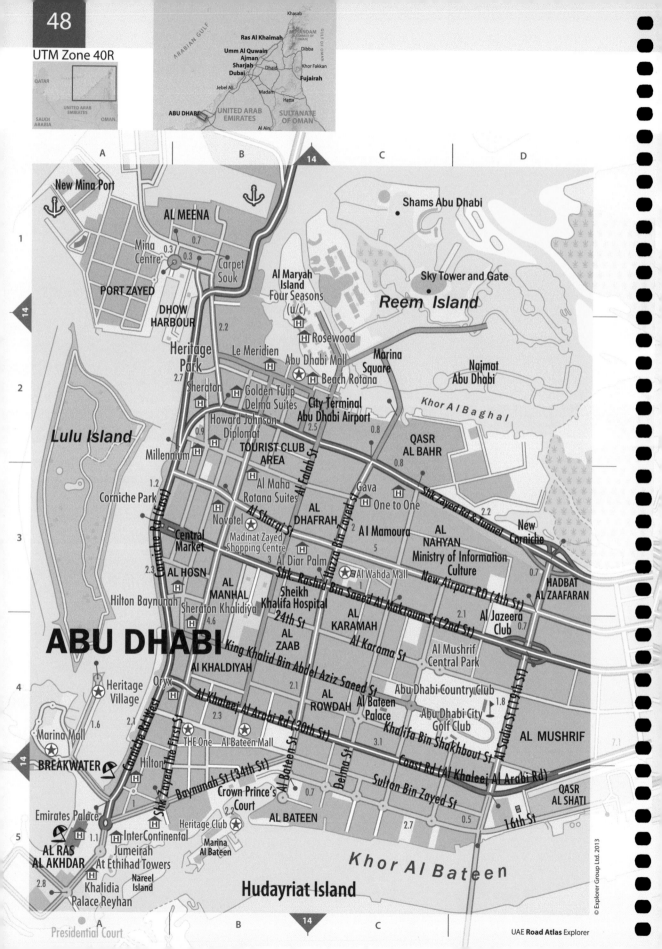

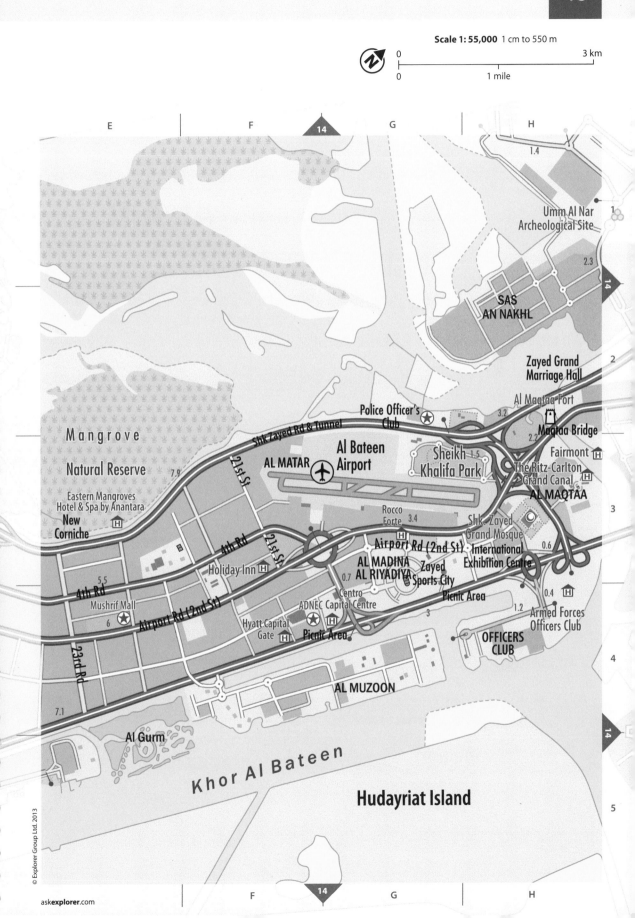

Scale 1:55,000 1 cm to 550 m

3 km

1 mile

Umm Al Nar
Archeological Site

1.4

2.3

SAS
AN NAKHL

Zayed Grand
Marriage Hall

Al Maqtaa Fort

3.2

Police Officer's
Club

Maqtaa Bridge

2.2

Shk Zayed Rd & Tunnel

AL MATAR

Al Bateen
Airport

Sheikh
Khalifa Park

1.5

Fairmont

The Ritz-Carlton
Grand Canal

AL MAQTAA

M a n g r o v e

Natural Reserve

7.9

Rocco
Forte

3.4

Shk Zayed
Grand Mosque

0.6

Eastern Mangroves
Hotel & Spa by Anantara

New
Corniche

21st St

21st St

4th Rd

Airport Rd (2nd St)

International
Exhibition Centre

AL MADINA
AL RIYADIYA

Zayed
Sports City

Picnic Area

0.4

Holiday Inn

Centro

5.5

0.7

1.2

Armed Forces
Officers Club

4th Rd

Mushrif Mall

6

Airport Rd (2nd St)

ADNEC Capital Centre

3

Hyatt Capital
Gate

Picnic Area

OFFICERS
CLUB

23rd Rd

7.1

AL MUZOON

Al Gurm

Khor Al Bateen

Hudayriat Island

UTM Zone 40R

UNITED ARAB
EMIRATES

Madinat
Zayed

Mazaira

SULTANATE
OF OMAN

QATAR

UNITED ARAB
EMIRATES

SAUDI
ARABIA

OMAN

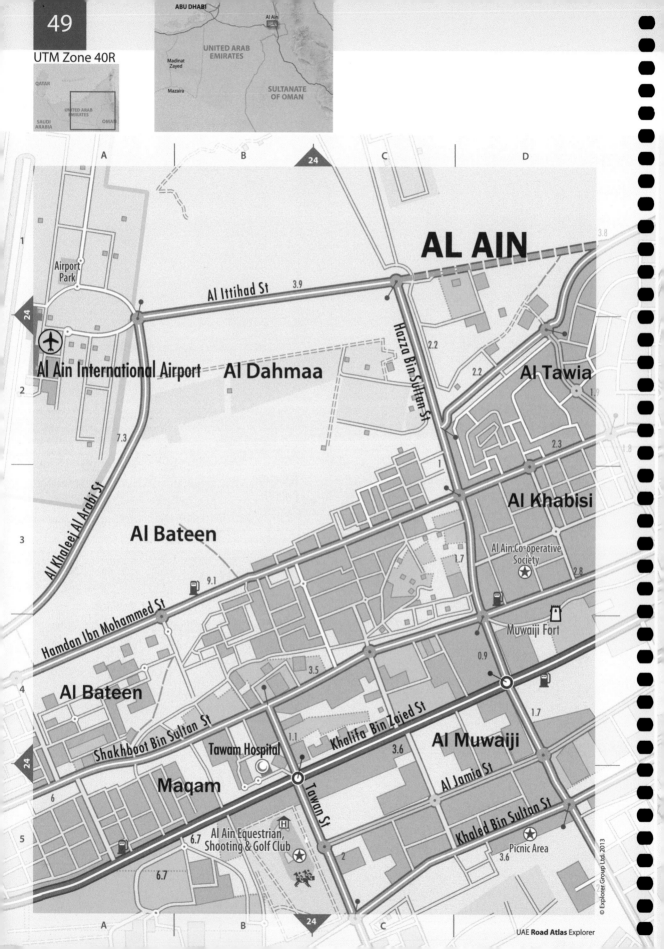

A   B   24   C   D

AL AIN

3.8

Airport
Park

Al Ittihad St   3.9

1

24

Al Ain International Airport   Al Dahmaa

2.2

2.2

Al Tawia

1.9

2

7.3

2.3

1.8

1

Al Khabisi

Al Bateen

3

Al Ain Co-operative
Society

2.8

1.7

9.1

Hamdan Ibn Mohammed St

Muwaiji Fort

0.9

4

Al Bateen

3.5

Shakhboot Bin Sultan St

Khalifa Bin Zajed St

1.7

Tawam Hospital

Al Muwaiji

1.1

3.6

Maqam

Al Jamia St

Tawan St

Khaled Bin Sultan St

5

6.7

Al Ain Equestrian,
Shooting & Golf Club

Picnic Area

3.6

2

6

24

6.7

Al Khaleej Al Arabi St

Hazza Bin Sultan St

A   B   24   C

© Explorer Group Ltd 2013

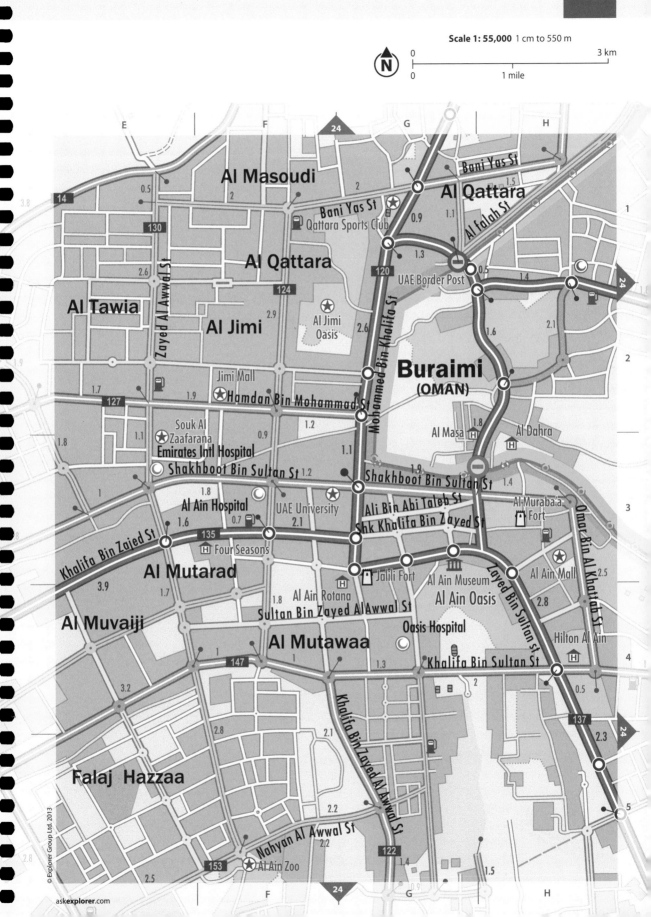

Scale 1: 55,000 1 cm to 550 m

N

0   3 km

0   1 mile

E   F   24   G   H

Al Masoudi

Bani Yas St

Al Qattara

Bani Yas St

Qattara Sports Club

Al falah St

1.5

1.1

0.9

Al Qattara

1.3

UAE Border Post

0.5

1.4

Al Tawia

Zayed Al Awwal St

Al Jimi

2.9

Al Jimi Oasis

2.6

1.6

2.1

Buraimi
(OMAN)

Mohammed Bin Khalifa St

Jimi Mall

Hamdan Bin Mohammad St

1.9

Al Masa

1.8

Al Dahra

127

1.8

1.1

Souk Al Zaafarana

0.9

1.2

Emirates Intl Hospital

Shakhboot Bin Sultan St 1.2

1.1

Shakhboot Bin Sultan St

1.4

1.9

Al Muraba'a Fort

Al Ain Hospital

1.8

UAE University

2.1

Ali Bin Abi Taleb St

Shk Khalifa Bin Zayed St

Omar Bin Al Khattab St

1.6

0.7

Four Seasons

Khalifa Bin Zaied St

135

Al Mutarad

Jalili Fort

Al Ain Museum

Al Ain Mall

2.5

Zayed Bin Sultan St

2.8

3.9

1.7

1.8

Al Ain Rotana

Al Ain Oasis

Hilton Al Ain

Al Muvaiji

Sultan Bin Zayed Al Awwal St

1

Al Mutawaa

Oasis Hospital

Khalifa Bin Sultan St

147

1

1.3

0.5

137

3.2

2

2.3

2.8

2.1

Falaj Hazzaa

Khalifa Bin Zayed Al Awwal St

2.2

2.2

Nahyan Al Awwal St

122

1.4

153

Al Ain Zoo

2.5

F   24   G   H

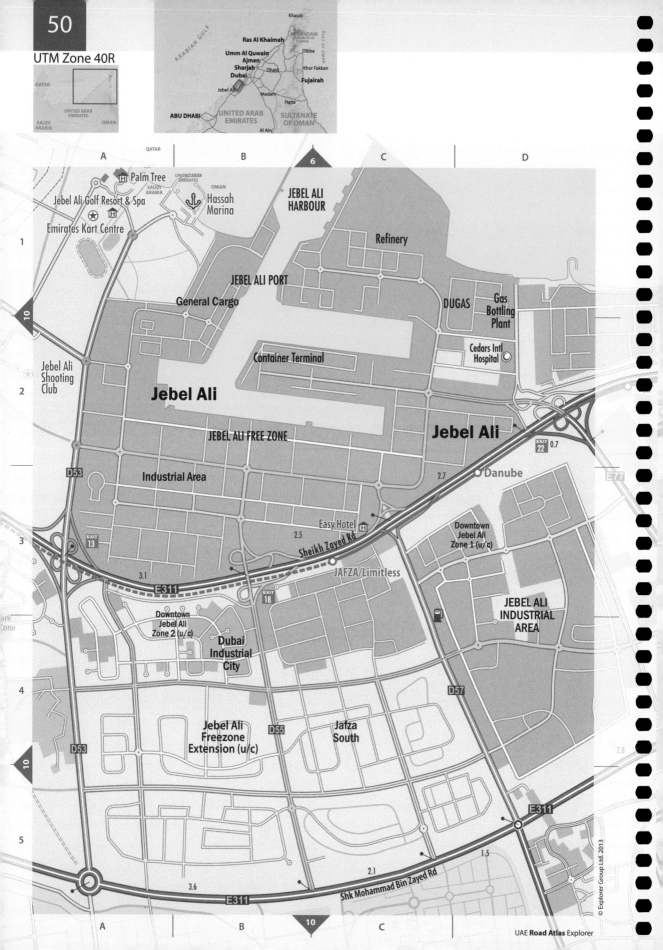

Scale 1: 55,000 1 cm to 550 m

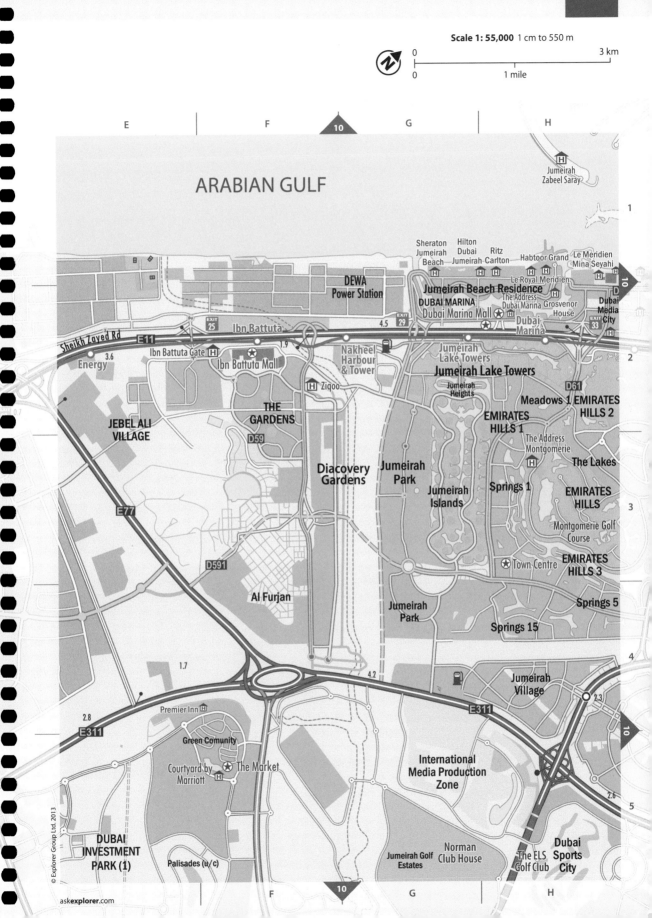

ARABIAN GULF

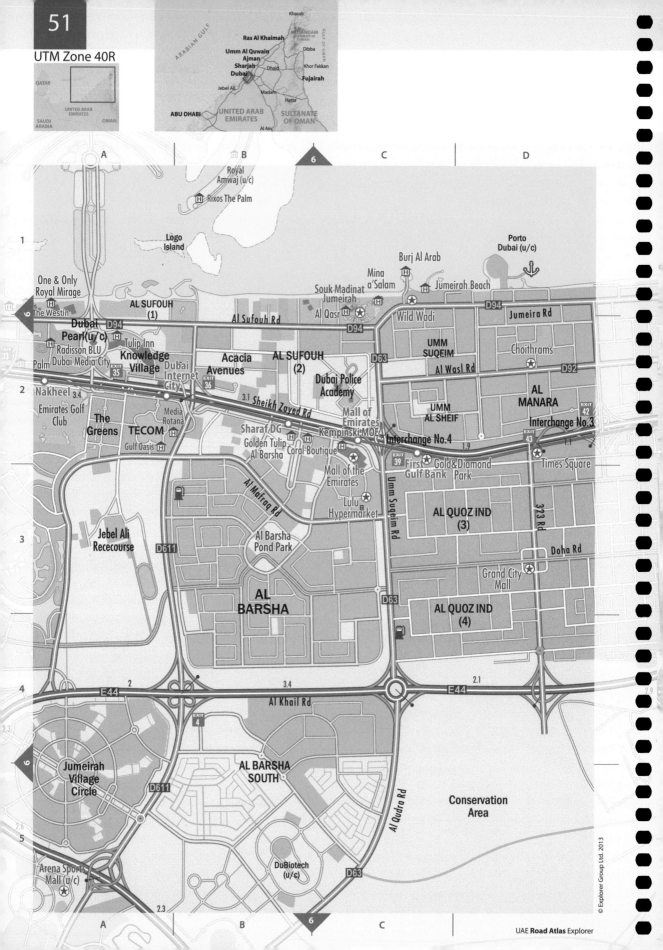

UTM Zone 40R

QATAR

UNITED ARAB
EMIRATES

SAUDI
ARABIA   OMAN

ARABIAN GULF

Khasab

Ras Al Khaimah

Umm Al Quwain
Ajman
Sharjah
Dubai

Jebel Ali

Madam

Dhaid

Dibba

Khor Fakkan

Fujairah

Hatta

ABU DHABI   UNITED ARAB
EMIRATES

Al Ain

SULTANATE
OF OMAN

GULF OF OMAN

A   **B**   6   **C**   **D**

Royal
Amwaj (u/c)

Rixos The Palm

1

Logo
Island

Porto
Dubai (u/c)

Burj Al Arab

Mina
a'Salam

Souk Madinat
Jumeirah

Jumeirah Beach

One & Only
Royal Mirage

The Westin

6

Al Qasr

Wild Wadi

D94   Jumeira Rd

**Dubai
Pearl(u/c)**   D94   Al Sufouh Rd   D94

Radisson BLU   Tulip Inn   **AL SUFOUH
(1)**

Palm Dubai Media City   **Knowledge
Village**

Nakheel 3.4

Emirates Golf
Club

**The
Greens**

TECOM

Gulf Oasis

**Dubai
Internet
City**

Media
Rotana

**Acacia
Avenues**

EXIT
36

3.1   Sheikh Zayed Rd

**AL SUFOUH
(2)**

Dubai Police
Academy

**UMM
SUQEIM**

Choithrams   D92

UMM
AL SHEIF

Al Wasl Rd

**AL
MANARA**

EXIT
42

Interchange No.3

EXIT
43

1.1

Mall of
Emirates   Interchange No.4   1.9

Kempinski MOE   First
Gulf Bank   Gold & Diamond
Park   **Times Square**

EXIT
39

Sharaf DG

Golden Tulip
Al Barsha   Coral Boutique

Mall of the
Emirates

**AL QUOZ IND
(3)**

323 Rd

Lulu
Hypermarket

Al Mafraq Rd

Doha Rd

3

Jebel Ali
Rececourse

D611

Al Barsha
Pond Park

Grand City
Mall

**AL
BARSHA**

D63

**AL QUOZ IND
(4)**

4   E44   2   3.4   E44   2.1

Al Khail Rd

EXIT
4

**Jumeirah
Village
Circle**

6

D611

**AL BARSHA
SOUTH**

Al Qudra Rd

**Conservation
Area**

5

Arena Sports
Mall (u/c)

DuBiotech
(u/c)

D63

2.3

A   **B**   6   **C**

© Explorer Group Ltd 2013

UAE **Road Atlas** Explorer

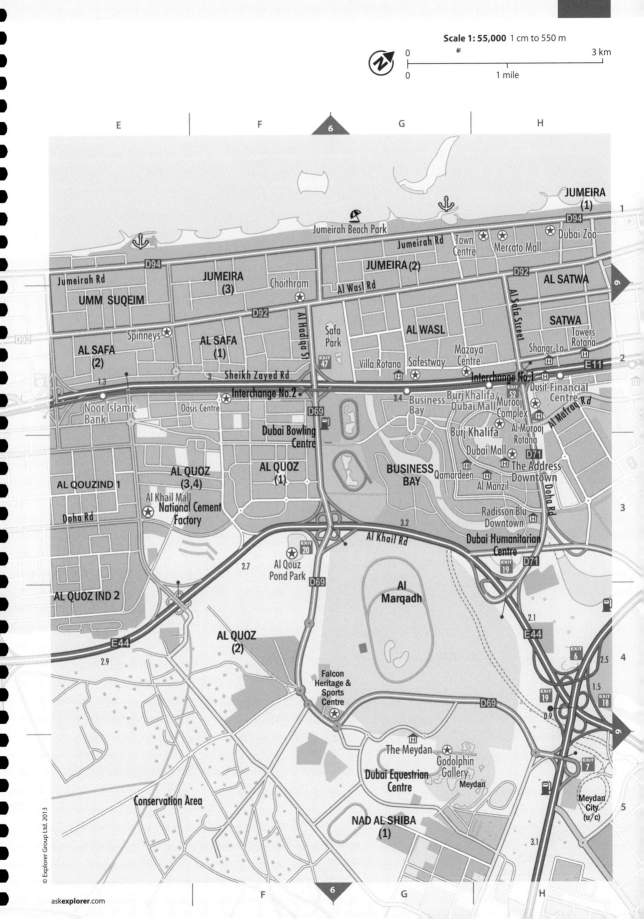

Scale 1: **55,000** 1 cm to 550 m

0   3 km
0   1 mile

JUMEIRA (1)

D94

Jumeirah Beach Park

Jumeirah Rd

Town Centre

Mercato Mall

Dubai Zoo

D94

JUMEIRA (3)

Choithram

JUMEIRA (2)

Al Wasl Rd

D92

AL SATWA

UMM SUQEIM

Jumeirah Rd

D92

Al Hadiqa St

Safa Park

AL WASL

Al Safa Street

SATWA

Shangr-La

Towers Rotana

Spinneys

AL SAFA (1)

Villa Rotana

Mazaya Centre

Safestway

AL SAFA (2)

1.3

EXIT 47

E11

D92

3   Sheikh Zayed Rd

Interchange No.1

Noor Islamic Bank

Oasis Centre

Interchange No.2

D69

3.4

Business Bay

Burj Khalifa/ Dubai Mall

Al Murooj Complex

Dusit Financial Centre

Al Mafraq Rd

Dubai Bowling Centre

EXIT 52

Al Murooj Rotana

AL QUOZ IND 1

AL QUOZ (3,4)

AL QUOZ (1)

Burj Khalifa

Dubai Mall

D71

Al Khail Mall

National Cement Factory

BUSINESS BAY

Qamardeen

The Address Downtown

Doha Rd

Al Manzil

Radisson Blu Downtown

Doha Rd

3

3.2

Dubai Humanitarian Centre

Al Khail Rd

D71

EXIT 20

EXIT 19

AL QUOZ IND 2

Al Qouz Pond Park

2.7

D69

Al Marqadh

2.1

E44

EXIT 6

2.5

E44

AL QUOZ (2)

2.9

Falcon Heritage & Sports Centre

1.5

EXIT 19

0.9

EXIT 18

D69

Conservation Area

The Meydan

Dubai Equestrian Centre

Godolphin Gallery

Meydan

EXIT 7

Meydan City (u/c)

NAD AL SHIBA (1)

3.1

© Explorer Group Ltd. 2013

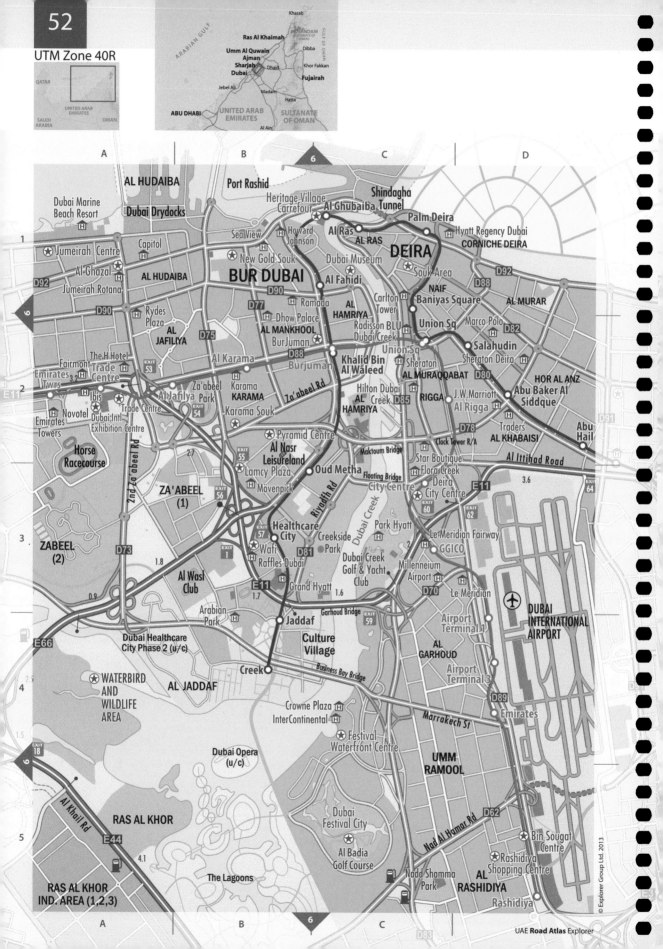

Scale 1: 55,000 1 cm to 550 m

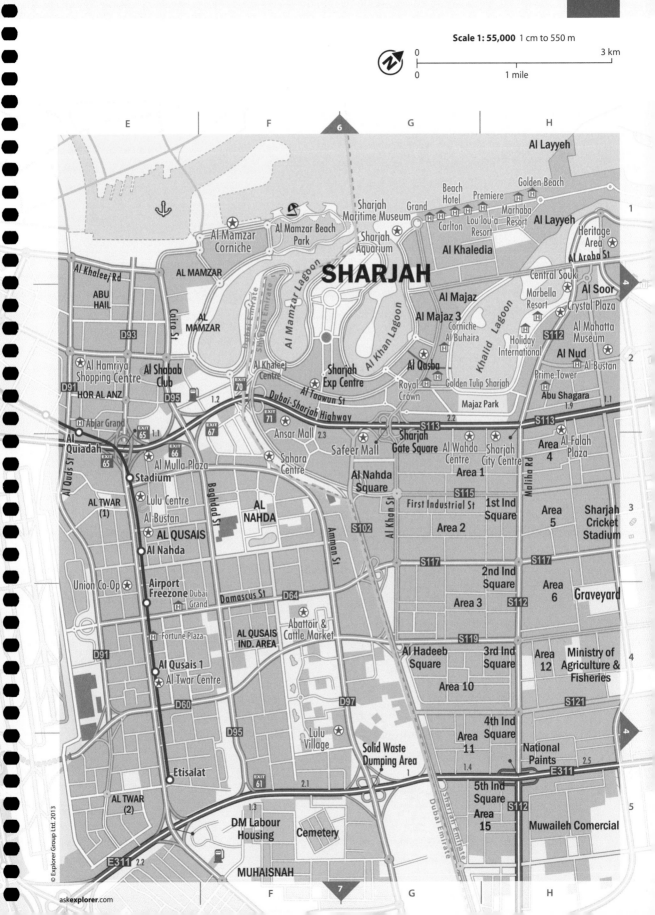

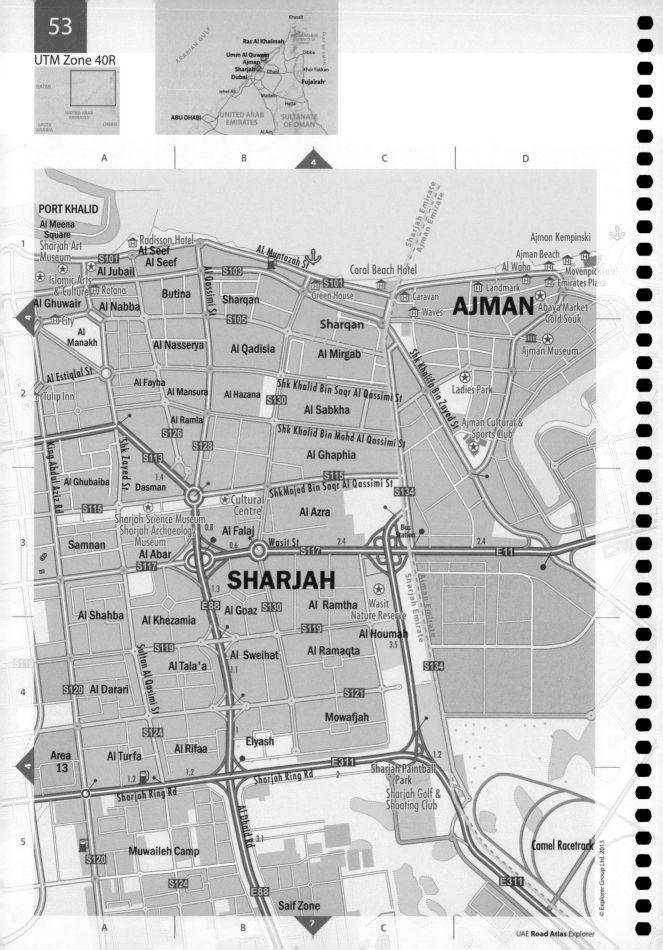

UTM Zone 40R

QATAR

UNITED ARAB EMIRATES

SAUDI ARABIA | OMAN

Khasab

ARABIAN GULF | MUSANDAM (SULTANATE OF OMAN) | GULF OF OMAN

Ras Al Khaimah

Dibba

Umm Al Quwain
Ajman
Sharjah
Dubai

Dhaid

Khor Fakkan

Fujairah

Jebel Ali | Madam

Hatta

ABU DHABI

UNITED ARAB EMIRATES

SULTANATE OF OMAN

Al Ain

A   **B**   **4**   **C**   **D**

PORT KHALID

Al Meena Square

Sharjah Art Museum

Radisson Hotel

Al Seef
Al Seef

AL Muntazah St

S101

Islamic Arts & Culture

Al Jubail

Rotana

Butina

Al Qassimi St

S103

Sharqan

S101

Green House

Coral Beach Hotel

Ajman Kempinski

Ajman Beach

Al Waha

Movenpick (u/c)

Emirates Plaza

Al Ghuwair

Al Nabba

City

Al Manakh

Al Estiqlal St

Tulip Inn

Al Fayha

Al Mansura

Al Ramla

Al Ghubaiba

Dasman

1.4

S115

Samnan

King Abdul Aziz Rd

Shk Zayed St

S126

S128

S113

S117

Al Abar

0.8

Cultural Centre

Al Falaj

0.6

Wasit St

S117

SHARJAH

Sharjah Science Museum
Sharjah Archaeology Museum

S105

Al Qadisia

Al Nasserya

Al Hazana

S130

Al Mirgab

Sharqan

Shk Khalid Bin Saqr Al Qassimi St

Al Sabkha

Shk Khalid Bin Mohd Al Qassimi St

Al Ghaphia

S115

ShkMajed Bin Saqr Al Qassimi St

Al Azra

2.4

Caravan

Waves

AJMAN

Abaya Market
Gold Soúk

Ajman Museum

Landmark

Ladies Park

Ajman Cultural & Sports Club

Shk Khalifa Bin Zayed St

S134

Bus Station

E11

2.4

Al Shahba

E88

Al Khezamia

S130

Al Goaz

Al Ramtha

Wasit Nature Reserve

S119

Al Houmah

3.5

S119

Al Tala'a

Al Sweihat

1.1

Al Ramaqta

Sultan Al Qassimi St

S120

Al Darari

S124

Area 13

Al Turfa

1.2

Al Rifaa

1.2

1.2

Elyash

S121

Mowafjah

Sharjah Ring Rd

Sharjah Ring Rd

E311

2

Sharjah Paintball Park

Sharjah Golf & Shooting Club

Al Dhaid Rd

3.1

Muwaileh Camp

S120

S124

E88

Saif Zone

7

Ajman Emirate

Sharjah Emirate

S134

1.2

Camel Racetrack

E311

© Explorer Group Ltd. 2013

UAE **Road Atlas** Explorer

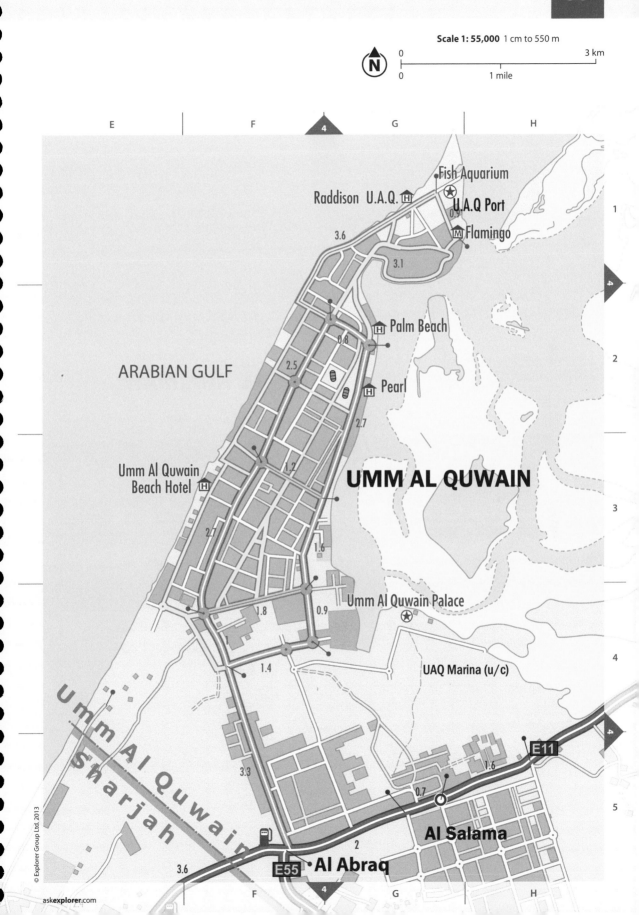

Scale 1: **55,000** 1 cm to 550 m

N

0   3 km
0   1 mile

E   F   4   G   H

Fish Aquarium

Raddison U.A.Q. H   ✪ U.A.Q Port   1

0.9

3.6   M Flamingo

3.1

4

H Palm Beach

0.8

2.5   ARABIAN GULF   2

H Pearl

2.7

1.2

UMM AL QUWAIN

Umm Al Quwain
Beach Hotel H   3

2.7

1.6

Umm Al Quwain Palace ✪

1.8   0.9

1.4   UAQ Marina (u/c)   4

E11

3.3   1.6

0.7   5

U m m A l Q u w a i n

S h a r j a h

2   **Al Salama**

3.6   E55   **Al Abraq**

F   4   G   H

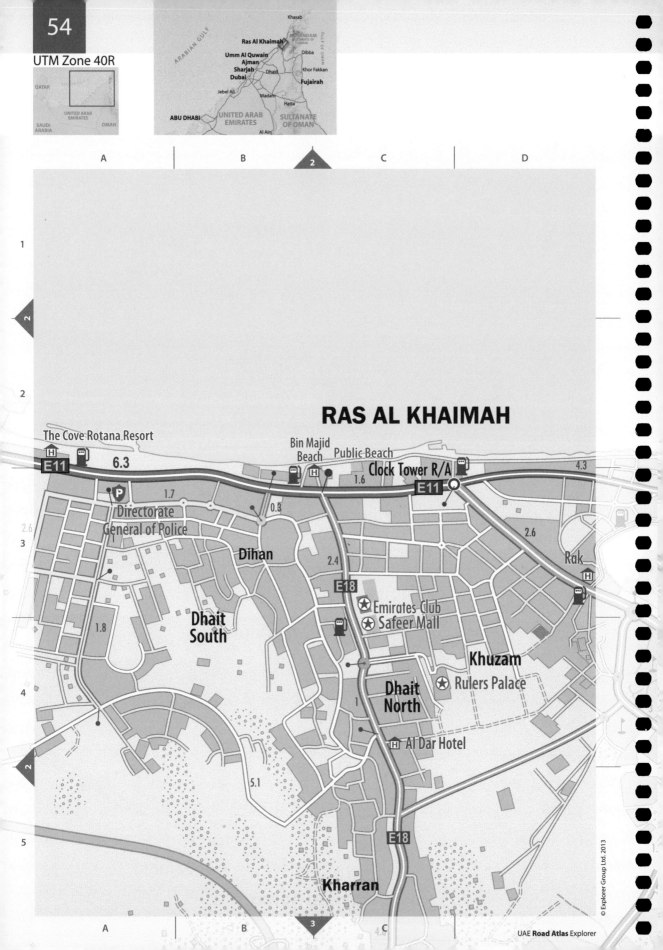

UTM Zone 40R

RAS AL KHAIMAH

The Cove Rotana Resort

E11   6.3

Bin Majid
Beach   Public Beach

Clock Tower R/A

E11   4.3

P
1.7

Directorate
General of Police

0.3

1.6

2.6

Dihan

2.4

Rak

E18

2.6

Emirates Club

Dhait
South

Safeer Mall

1.8

Khuzam

Rulers Palace

Dhait
North

1

Al Dar Hotel

5.1

E18

Kharran

4.6

© Explorer Group Ltd. 2013

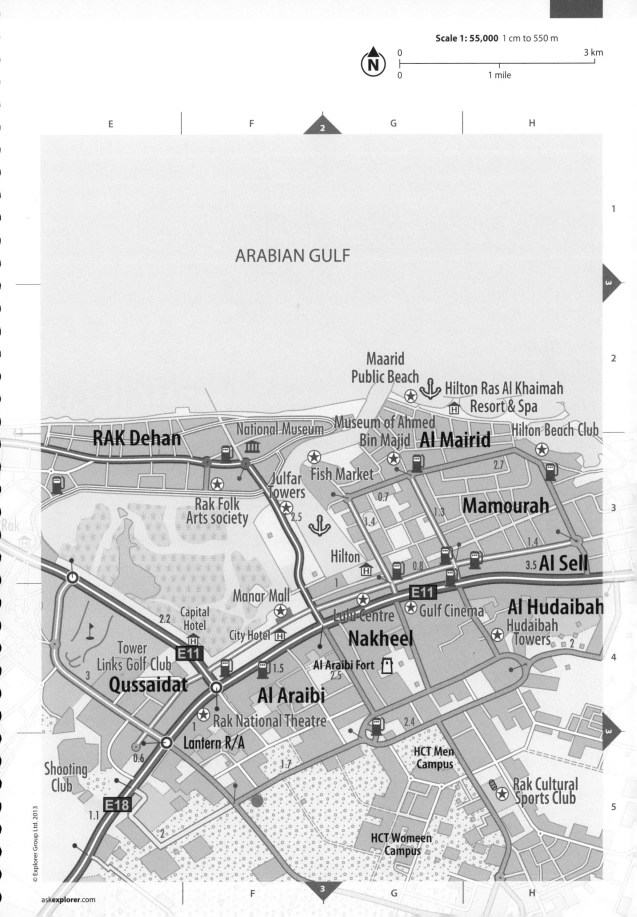

N

0   3 km

0   1 mile

ARABIAN GULF

Maarid
Public Beach

Hilton Ras Al Khaimah
Resort & Spa

Hilton Beach Club

RAK Dehan

National Museum

Museum of Ahmed
Bin Majid

Al Mairid

Fish Market

Julfar
Towers

Rak Folk
Arts society

2.5

0.7

Mamourah

1.3

1.4

1.4

Hilton

0.8

3.5 **Al Sell**

1

Manar Mall

Capital
Hotel

2.2

City Hotel

Lulu Centre

Gulf Cinema

Nakheel

Al Hudaibah

Hudaibah
Towers

2

Tower
Links Golf Club

E11

3

Al Araibi Fort

2.5

1.5

Qussaidat

Al Araibi

Rak National Theatre

1

2.4

Lantern R/A

0.6

Shooting
Club

E18

1.7

HCT Men
Campus

Rak Cultural
Sports Club

1.1

2

HCT Womeen
Campus

© Explorer Group Ltd. 2013

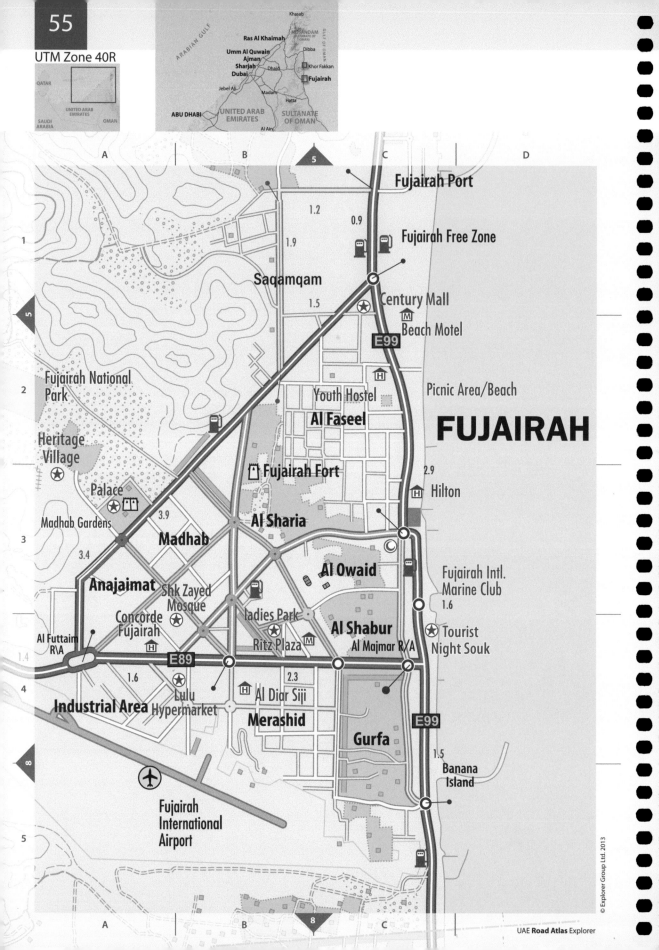

UTM Zone 40R

QATAR

UNITED ARAB
EMIRATES

SAUDI
ARABIA   OMAN

ARABIAN GULF

Khasab

MUSANDAM
(SULTANATE OF OMAN)

GULF OF OMAN

Ras Al Khaimah

Umm Al Quwain
Ajman
Sharjah
Dubai

Dibba

Dhaid

Khor Fakkan

Fujairah

Jebel Ali

Madam

Hatta

ABU DHABI

UNITED ARAB
EMIRATES

SULTANATE
OF OMAN

Al Ain

A   B   5   C   D

Fujairah Port

1.2   0.9

1.9   **Fujairah Free Zone**

Saqamqam

1.5   **Century Mall**

E99   **Beach Motel**

1   5   2

Youth Hostel   Picnic Area/Beach

Al Faseel   **FUJAIRAH**

🏰 Fujairah Fort   2.9

Hilton

Heritage Village

Palace

Madhab Gardens   3.9

3.4   **Madhab**   **Al Sharia**

Al Owaid

Anajaimat   Fujairah Intl.
Marine Club   1.6

Shk Zayed
Mosque   ladies Park

Concorde
Fujairah   Ritz Plaza   **Al Shabur**   **Tourist
Night Souk**

Al Futtaim
R\A   E89   Al Majmar R\A

1.4   1.6   2.3   **Al Diar Siji**

Industrial Area   Lulu
Hypermarket   **Merashid**

E99

Gurfa

1.5

**Banana
Island**

**Fujairah
International
Airport**

A   B   8   C

© Explorer Group Ltd 2013

UAE **Road Atlas** Explorer

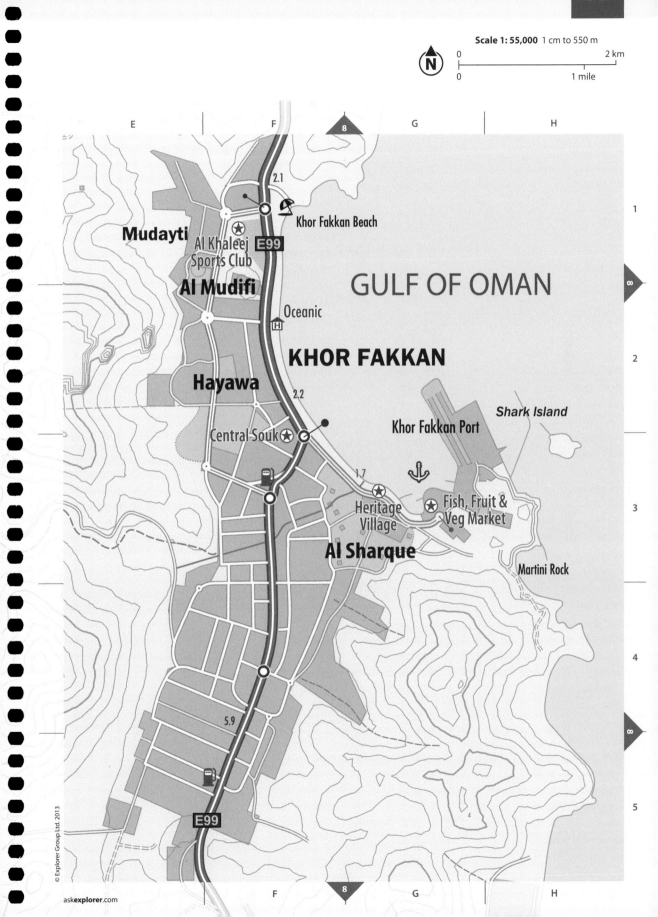

Scale 1: **55,000** 1 cm to 550 m

N

0 _____ 2 km

0 _____ 1 mile

E   F   8   G   H

2.1

Khor Fakkan Beach

Mudayti

Al Khaleej
Sports Club

E99

Al Mudifi

Oceanic

GULF OF OMAN

KHOR FAKKAN

Hayawa

2.2

Shark Island

Central Souk

Khor Fakkan Port

1.7

Fish, Fruit &
Veg Market

Heritage
Village

Al Sharque

Martini Rock

5.9

E99

© Explorer Group Ltd. 2013

AUH – Abu Dhabi
AJM – Ajman
DXB – Dubai
FUJ – Fujairah
KSA - Saudi Arabia
OMN – Oman
RAK – Ras Al Khaimah
SHJ – Sharjah
UAQ – Umm Al Quwain

This index is not an authority on administrative or international boundaries

C

D

E

F

G

H

N

O

P

S

T

U

Explorer Products

Residents' Guides

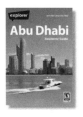 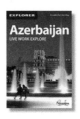   

Mini Visitors' Guides

Photography Books & Calendars

Maps

Adventure & Lifestyle Guides

UAE Road Atlas Team

Project Manager	Alistair MacKenzie
Cartography Manager	Zain Madathil
Cartography Team	Noushad Madathil, Dhanya Nellikkunnummal
Editor	Carli Allan

Publishing
Publisher Alistair MacKenzie
Associate Publisher Claire England

Editorial
Managing Editor – Consumer Carli Allan
Guides Editor Jo Iivonen
Deputy Guides Editor Stacey Siebritz
Managing Editor – Corporate Charlie Scott
Deputy Corporate Editor Lily Lawes
Digital Projects Editor Rachel McArthur
Web Editor Laura Coughlin
Production Assistant Vanessa Eguia
Editorial Assistant Amapola Castillo
Researchers Farida, Jagadeesh, Praseena Kunnummal, Shalu M Sukumaran, Roja P

Design & Photography
Creative Director Pete Maloney
Art Director Ieyad Charaf
Designer Michael Estrada
Junior Designer M. Shakkeer
Layout Manager Jayde Fernandes
Cartography Manager Zain Madathil
Cartographers Noushad Madathil, Dhanya Nellikkunnummal, Ramla Kambravan, Gayathri CM
GIS Analysts Rafi KM, Hidayath Razi, Mohamed Aslam
Photography Manager Pamela Grist
Photographer Bart Wojcinski
Image Library Jyothin Thekkiniyedath

Sales & Marketing
Group Media Sales Manager Peter Saxby
Media Sales Area Managers Laura Zuffova, Sabrina Ahmed, Bryan Anes, Adam Smith, Louise Burton, Matthew Whitbread
Business Development Manager Pouneh Hafizi
Corporate Solutions Account Manager Vibeke Nurgberg
Group Marketing & PR Manager Lindsay West
Senior Marketing Executive Stuart L. Cunningham
Group Retail Sales Manager Ivan Rodrigues
Retail Sales Coordinator Michelle Mascarenhas
Retail Sales Area Supervisors Ahmed Mainodin, Firos Khan
Retail Sales Merchandisers Johny Mathew, Shan Kumar
Retail Sales Drivers Shabsir Madathil, Najumudeen K.I., Sujeer Khan
Warehouse Assistant Mohamed Haji

Finance & Administration
Accountant Cherry Enriquez
Accounts Assistants Sunil Suvarna, Joy Bermejo Belza, Jeanette Carino Enecillo
Admin Assistant & Reception Joy H. San Buenaventura
Public Relations Officer Rafi Jamal
Office Assistant Shafeer Ahamed
Office Manager – India Jithesh Kalathingal

IT & Digital Solutions
Digital Solutions Manager Derrick Pereira
IT Administrator R. Ajay
Database Programmer Pradeep T.P.

Contact Us

General Enquiries
We'd love to hear your thoughts and answer any questions you have about this book or any other Explorer product. Contact us at **info@askexplorer.com**

Careers
If you fancy yourself as an Explorer, send your CV (stating the position you're interested in) to **jobs@askexplorer.com**

Contract Publishing
For enquiries about Explorer's Contract Publishing arm and design services contact **contracts@askexplorer.com**

PR & Marketing
For PR and marketing enquiries contact **marketing@askexplorer.com**

Corporate Sales & Licensing
For bulk sales and customisation options, for this book or any Explorer product, contact **sales@askexplorer.com**

Advertising & Sponsorship
For advertising and sponsorship, contact **sales@askexplorer.com**

Explorer Publishing & Distribution
PO Box 34275, Dubai, United Arab Emirates
www.askexplorer.com

Phone: +971 (0)4 340 8805
Fax: +971 (0)4 340 8806